Long before Mark Zuckerberg started taking over the universe, one friend request at a time, *Pure Derry* lived on an old-fashioned website. One that was lovingly hand-built with good ol' HTML pages, dodgy blue links, animated GIFs and one of those groovy hit counters that went up by one every time someone came knocking.

And they did: over 750,000 times, across 41 editions, between 2003 and 2007. The poor bastards ...

Pure Derry returned to the world of men in the shape of a Facebook page in the summer of 2012. Freed from the shackles of producing time-consuming 'editions', the editor (it is rumoured) now simply writes stuff during his lunch break, hits post and goes back to work. Others claim he gets £1 from Bill Gates every time someone shares a post.

Pure Derry now has over fifteen thousand fans on Facebook and is known to a new generation of readers, who were probably too busy playing with Power Rangers to pay much attention last time out.

This book is all our best bits (not necessarily in chronological order); the jokes, stories and features that you've laughed at, objected to, commented on and shared over the last ten years.

Pure Derry

BLACKSTAFF PRESS

First published in 2013 by
Blackstaff Press
4D Weavers Court
Linfield Road
Belfast
BT12 5GH

with the assistance of
The Arts Council of Northern Ireland

Designed by seagulls.net
Printed and bound by GraphyCEMS

ISBN 978 0 85640 919 6

www.blackstaffpress.com
www.facebook.com/PureDerry

Contents

New Year's resolution: read more — 6

Horoscopes — 10

The difficult second edition — 12

All you need is love. Cash would help too. — 16

Jobs — 20

The Vantastic Four — 22

Classifieds — 26

Happy Saint Paddy's Day — 28

Different horses for different main courses — 32

Birdman & Booster Seat — 36

Don't put all your taigs in one basket — 38

Republican Action Against Something Or Other — 42

Derry album chart — 46

May the fourth be with you — 48

Welcome to summer. T-shirts optional. — 52

Radio One Big Weekend Newsfeed — 56

The sun is shining and the weather is sweet, to the beat — 58

The Twelfth edition — 62

Summer loving, had me a blast. (Still a bit stoned, tbh!) — 68

Derry movie chart — 72

Too cool for school (well, on a Sat and Sun anyway) — 76

Take your oil, hi. Emergency drums starting from £15. — 80

Funnies — 84

Red and white army — 86

Happy Hallowe'en — 90

Majella's mailbag — 94

Pure decommissioning — 96

It would freeze the balls off a brass monkey — 100

It's beginning to look a lot like Christmas — 104

50 things to do in Derry — 108

Thanks — 120

Pure Derry

New Year's Resolution: Read More

News shorts

Derry has come fourth in the *Best in Travel 2013* guide published by Lonely Planet. Support came from all over the world, from as far away as China and South America. Voters such as Ting Xu Doherty and Jesus-Ernesto McLaughlin are said to be delighted with the result.

Bad news for the travelling public today, as Translink confirmed that the Derry to Coleraine line will be closed for nine months for essential maintenance.

In even worse news, the Road Service has confirmed that the road to Strabane will remain open indefinitely.

John Hume spends whole day opening bags of crisps for the elderly. 'I did it for one person, and suddenly a big queue started to form. I only did what anyone else would have. For nine hours.'

NEW 'RIVER' INSTALLATION HAILED A SUCCESS

Derry City Council staff met in secret this morning to participate in a closed-doors group high-fiving session after the remarkable success of the recent Clipper sailing event.

Derry people were delighted to wake up last week to find that city chiefs had pumped billions of gallons of water into the centre of town, creating what's known as a 'river', which flows right through the city.

The ambitious scheme, which other cities have used successfully for years, follows the principle that its 'kinda nice' to do stuff along the waterfront other than park cars, dispose of shopping trolleys and hire out floor sanders.

The spectacular event has galvanised the city ahead of the imminent 2013 celebrations, with tens of thousands turning out to see off the Clippers on the last leg of their voyage to end a brilliant week for Derry.

It wasn't all plain sailing though. Local boat *Derry-Londonderry* initially looked in trouble after several crew members fell ill before casting off. However local actress, singer and yacht master Bronagh Gallagher kindly stepped in to help out.

'She was always a very talented helmsman and navigator at school,' said her agent.

Despite concerns, local mafia group, Repulsive Activities After Dark, didn't spoil the event, with intel from MI5 indicating that both members were off doing a fag run to Santa Ponsa.

Other headlines

Foyle Search and Rescue temporarily forced to shut as keys to the boat are lost.

Real centre of universe found. Derry women in shock.

Gun panic at Derry pub as clueless barman misunderstands boss's instruction to give out free shots.

PHIL COULTER IN TOWN ADULTERY SHOCKER

Derry citizens everywhere were shocked and saddened to hear of Phil Coulter's adultery this week when, after a sudden raid on the Coulter estate, police found a number of songs professing love for any number of other towns and cities.

The discovery of 'I Heartily Approve Of You, Milton Keynes', 'Bristol-Whipped' and 'Three Cheers For Ipswich', among others, has led the PSNI to question the seventy-one-year-old songwriter and stuntman.

Lines such as 'I never knew a town fairer/ Than Weston-super-Mare, ah!' led angry police chiefs to publicly accuse Coulter of having pursued a ruthless campaign of infidelity for more than twenty-seven years. Coulter, who for forty years has insisted that Derry is the one and only

town in his heart, initially denied allegations of a string of affairs with other towns, cities and the principalities of Monaco and the Vatican City. However, in a change of heart, he later owned up to the shameful events, appealing directly to the people of the city for their forgiveness.

'They meant nothing to me, those places. You don't know what it's like on the road – suddenly everyone wants a piece of you, and it's so easy to give into temptation. Derry, you were always my number one and I would never have said, sung or written anything to hurt you. I was drunk and lonely. I'm really sorry.'

Lines recovered from his song 'Hmmmmmm, Stockport!' seem to contradict this claim, however: 'When I got off the ferry/ From that shithole Derry/ I found that Stockport/ Was an altogether more affable and interesting place in which to live.'

Even more sickening is the fact that each of the 496 other cities appear to have been completely unaware of his infidelity. Bradford mayor John Bradford said

in a statement released last night, 'We are saddened and devastated to hear this news of Phil Coulter's adultery. It's hard to believe that

we mean nothing to him. We feel like such fools.'

Bradford added, 'We, as a community, must move on and re-evaluate our relationship with Coulter. Coming after all his years of famously calling us "the town he loved so great", this will not be easy to do. But we will strive to put this behind us.'

On hearing the news, Pope Benedict XVI lost hope in humanity and handed in his resignation.

NEW NI BACK-TO-WORK SCHEME NOT WORKING, SAY PEOPLE WHO ACTUALLY WORK

Northern Ireland taxpayers are finally getting to see their hard-earned tax pounds put to use, as thousands of people who get paid for not having a job continue to work at bringing down the economy.

Meanwhile, those who get paid to keep the economy running failed to turn up for work for the eighteenth day running.

The controversial 'Our Time, Our Place' back-to-work scheme, which has been in operation now since 3 December 2012, requires loyalist dole claimants, more used to waiting around for their number to be called, to support a new alternative approach of refusing to believe when their number is up.

It remains unconfirmed if the huge salaries of work-shy MLAs will be divided out amongst the protesters, who have been working tirelessly to reinstate fascism in the halls of power in their absence. None of the politicians, not a

single one of them, had anything to say on the matter at all.

Everyone remained unavailable for comment, indefinitely.

'Silence in the courtyard, silence in the streets. The biggest mouth in Stormont's just about to speak,' said First Minister Peter Robinson when he kicked off a festive game of cross-unionist 'Who Can Go The Longest Without Speaking' nearly three weeks ago up on the Hill.

Meanwhile, the PSNI, the publicly financed strong arm of the law, upheld its commitment to keep the local community safe by providing weak-fingered real-time Twitter updates about how little its officers are actually doing.

Sport

DERRY SNOOKER TABLE SHORTAGE CONTINUES

Snooker clubs in the North West are in crisis today, as news emerges of a citywide shortage of snooker tables at clubs all over the Foyle area.

It is believed that the shortage is linked to a supply problem at the manufacturers, as the wood used to build snooker tables is the same as that used in the creation of dado rails and cheap laminate flooring.

Packie McGarvey of North West

Snooker voiced his concern about the shortage, fearing that it could bring the city's snooker league to its knees. 'It's a disgrace,' said Packie. 'We all have to share one table and no one has a clue whose shot it is next. It's not so bad when you get down to the colours, but when big Danny is on the beers and everyone is trying to hit the cue ball at once it's a real nightmare.'

There is now a fear within the Foyle snooker community that this shortage could force the upcoming Creggan snooker festival to be cancelled. Joe Quigley of the Foyle Snooker Community Association said, 'This shortage could force the upcoming Creggan snooker festival to be cancelled.'

Dear Majella,
I've started putting on a bit of weight in recent months, and I think it's really starting to bother my husband. I bought two different Atkins books a few months ago, and despite reading them both several times, I haven't lost ANY weight at all.

Anyway, I decided that I would start my own diet and see how it went, and I have to admit, I've been really good lately. For starters, I only buy a small packet of chocolate digestives now for having with my tea instead of the big pack I would normally have bought. Now I know what you are thinking: chocolate isn't good for you, but I'm no slouch, Majella, I lick all the chocolate off the biscuits before I sit down for my cuppa, meaning I save lots of calories. It's just like having NORMAL DIGESTIVES!!

My mother has also been telling me that it's not good to send out to Bridie's chippy every night for dinner, so I've taken her advice and started eating Ryvita and tuna fish crackers at teatime. This is really handy, because it tides me over lovely til I wait for Mickey to make the longer drive over the Golden Fryer in the Waterside instead. Have you heard similar bad reports about Bridie's? I wonder what the matter is!! I have been buying in

DERRY'S #1 AGONY AUNT

lots and lots of diet yogurts, Go Ahead bars and Weight Watchers microwave meals, but no matter how many of them I eat (I mean I don't even like yogurt but I force myself) I never seem to lose a pound. It's really frying my head, Majella. Nothing I do seems to work and me heart is broke!

Worse than that, I'm out a fortune and I just can't keep up with all this for much longer. I'm that bad for money now, I was even considering doing a few hours part-time work in the wee shop round the corner, but I worked out that it wouldn't be worth my while after I paid for taxis there and back, so I didn't

bother. The bastards are charging £2 minimum fare now, ye know – it's a fuckin' disgrace. Anyway Majella, I need your help, what can I do???
Love
Donna, Creggan

Majella says

Ack luv, we've all been there, and sometimes the oul diets are hard to get right. My advice would be to get in some exercise when you can – it's the only surefire way to shift the flab. Now I know what you're thinking – 'I haven't got the time for fancy exercising' – and I understand this (you don't have to tell me how good the daytime TV shows are!!). But there are some easy exercises that us independent, free-thinking, intellectual and empowered women of Derry can work into our busy schedules and daily routines to shift the weight.

Some of the exercises that I personally use to stay shipshape include beating around the bush, dodging the issue, hiding the truth, taking a hike, jumping to conclusions, moving the goalposts, running around in circles, side-stepping the issue and carrying the weight of the world on my shoulders. They are really good, and no one will even know that you are getting exercise!
Majella

Aries

Fortune favours you this week when you find an unused shipping container down the back of the sofa. Knowing a good business opportunity when you see one, you convert it into a shop and relocate it to a busy Galliagh roadside.

Taurus

A visit from an old friend cheers you up this week when they tell you some great news. Their life has turned out even worse than yours! Reinvigorated by the wonder of existence, you tap your Ma for a sub to head out.

Gemini

Lady Luck shines on you this week when you find a tenner in an old pair of jeans that you were about to wash. Your luck turns, however, when your electric runs out at the very second you realise you've no washing powder. Another £3 should cover it.

Cancer

A group of friends suggest you organise a trip to a fortune-teller. Unconvinced, you pour scorn on the idea and tell them you don't believe in all that crap. Good call. Don't waste your money on mumbo jumbo.

Leo

An urge to be more green-fingered takes hold of you in the coming days and you decide to do a bit of gardening. After intense negotiations on your doorstep, you pay two teenagers £4 to cut your disgracefully long grass with a dubious looking petrol powered strimmer, then spend the rest of the week moaning that they never cleaned up after themselves. Still, that's that for another year!

Virgo

Heartbreak lies ahead for you, when you discover you haven't won the EuroMillions again. You spend three days in bed in mourning.

HOROSCOPES

Libra

Pressure at work will get to you this week and you mistakenly put an extra sugar in your tea. You confide in your colleague about your error, but they don't seem to care. Feeling no one respects your opinion you immediately begin looking for a new job. You'll show those bastards!!

Scorpio

A taxi man recognises your face this week because of a passing resemblance to an uncle you've only met twice. You spend an extra five minutes parked in a lay-by talking about him despite the fact you are running late and your Da thinks he's a dick.

Sagittarius

The words of someone you barely know will leave you mystified this week during an important telephone call. When the fuck did AXA set up a car insurance call centre in Ballymena?

Capricorn

You get some very bad news when a romance comes to an end. Inside you are hurting, badly. However, you hide it well in front of others when you only post twenty-seven times on Facebook to reassure everyone that you are getting on with your life.

Aquarius

Romance is in the air this week when you see the girl of your dreams eating a cheesy chip in Jungle King. You try to impress her with your prowess on the teddy bear machine but she's not interested in guys for their cool stuff and bling. You need a new plan!

Pisces

Car troubles hamper your week when you break down on the way to work. Stranded, cold and alone at the side of the road, you realise you've no smokes left. Total nightmare. Thankfully someone opens a shop inside a shipping container 10ft away from you selling extremely reasonably priced cigarettes.

Pure Derry

The Difficult Second Edition

Following last night's digital switchover, the BBC has announced that it is to open a support hotline to help Derrymen traumatised by the demise of the Ceefax teletext service. Health centres across the city are said to be filling up with denim-clad forty-year-olds in deep distress, clutching bookie dockets and old remote controls.

The PSNI has confirmed that army technical officers have made safe two viable explosive devices at the riverside City Council offices. Following the scare, a team of 'special consultants' from the corner of John Street are now being brought in due to their vast experience in getting bombed up the quay.

Loyalist flag protesters are continuing in their quest to 'Not be the generation which fails Ulster' by continuing to be the generation which fails Ulster. 'It's not fair,' said Willie McFleggerson from Sandy Row. 'We're getting treated like Taigs by the police these days! We didn't expect equal rights to be this equal,' he moaned when someone mentioned the Good Friday Agreement.

GIVE PEACE BRIDGE A CHANCE

Following the success of the Peace Bridge, citysiders have today welcomed new plans to build additional bridges across the Foyle, admitting that going to the Waterside was 'not as bad as they expected'.

'You couldn't have paid me to go to the Waterside before,' said Sock-fluff McKeever from Creggan. 'But I took the wains over to that 100 per cent free Peace One concert and they had a ball. I got the free tickets on eBay for a score each. Delighted!!'

Next year, the new Ebrington arena will host over 40 live concerts as part of the 2013 celebrations. Bronagh Gallagher, who is reportedly headlining all of them, was unable to speak to our reporter as she is busy designing the New-New-New Bridge.

'She was always a very talented architect at school,' said a source.

CITY IN SHOCK FOLLOWING LOCAL MAN'S ASTONISHING DISCOVERY

Following the news that scientists in the USA have pioneered a revolutionary cure for AIDS, another astonishing story broke today, causing shockwaves across the city.

Witnesses claim that a local driver has miraculously discovered a way to make the sides of his car 'light up' as he turns a corner.

The amazing incident, which some cynics are still dismissing as a 'fantastical conspiracy theory', is reported to have taken place early yesterday morning at the Branch Road roundabout. Up to a dozen workers at the nearby HML offices claim to have seen 'a weird flashing orange glow' from outside as they were pretending to work.

Although frightened, one brave employee plucked up the courage to approach the window, just in time to see a blue Toyota Corolla exit the roundabout as it emitted a strange orange light.

'It was incredible,' he told our reporter during his tea break while he calmed his nerves with a pasta-filled toasted bap inside in a buttered crusty baguette. 'It was like I knew what way the car was going to go … before it even went there!!! I've never seen anything like it.'

As word of the feat spread, curious locals eventually managed to track down the driver, eager to know what special modifications he had made to the vehicle. However, they were stunned to learn that the car was unaltered in any way: news that has rocked the local academic community.

Car historians at Magee College have often speculated that the mysterious 'spare lever' above the driving wheel was once used by our non-psychic driving ancestors for a now long-forgotten purpose. Until now, however, such theories have been considered dangerous territory – and those who put them forward have often found their careers brought to an abrupt end.

Disgraced professor Charles Mackenzie, who was fired by the University of Ulster in 2004 for publicly claiming it was possible to park a BMW without taking up two parking spaces, was ecstatic at the news. 'I knew it!' he shouted. 'I'll show those bastards at Magee that I was right about everything!'

Local taxi drivers have also been shocked by the news. 'I can't believe it goes up and down, as well as in and out!!' said Lambert McButler from Foyle Delta Cabs, when he was told about the magic lever. 'I thought it was just for flashing the lights at junctions to let good-looking women out.'

Other headlines

Investigation launched as BT engineer's laptop is stolen in Rossville Street. 'We know the thief's name but, sadly, his number's ex-directory,' say PSNI.

Outrage as Ballymac kids as young as five stone buses. 'I'm shocked,' said one mother, 'I only turned away for a few hours to watch Jeremy Kyle, and then suddenly this happens.'

Local irony fans delighted as fat people across the city rush to join 'Boot' camps in effort to look better.

STRABANE WRISTBAND ANNOUNCED

Derry's corner shops announced today that the long-awaited Strabane wristband would soon be on sale citywide.

Due to popular demand, the wristband has been developed specifically for the Derry market, as charitable Derry folk persistently attempt to help the poor town out.

'We were getting requests for these wristbands literally four or five times an hour,' claims local shopkeeper Myra, of Creggan. 'They'd want cancer or multiple sclerosis or autism as well, yeah, but the Strabane requests kept flooding in. On a few occasions we've completely sold out of them!'

Over the last few weeks, shopkeepers and staff have reported a growing feeling of agitation among Derry's population about Strabane and concern over what to do about its sufferers.

'I suppose the feeling of many concerned Derry folk like me was, you know, "out of sight out of mind". If you're not from Strabane, maybe you wouldn't be aware of just how terrible it is,' says John O'Neill, of Strabane-Aid, the foundation currently selling the wristbands.

'With this product, however, you're not just showing solidarity with the people of Strabane, you're also spreading awareness of Strabane, and that's an important step towards what we want, which is a full cure for Strabane within the next ten to twenty years.'

Scientists say such a cure is a long way off, but applaud the foundation's attempts. 'A cure for Strabane isn't likely any time soon. Anyone familiar with sufferers of Moville will be aware of that finding a cure is a long process, but the wristband is a step in the right direction, and who knows, if it's successful, we might be talking of a breakthrough in the next decade.'

At the time of publishing, as many as twenty thousand people are estimated to be suffering from Strabane.

Dear Majella

DERRY'S #1 AGONY AUNT

Dear Majella,

I hope you can help me because I'm at my wits' end. I am really worried that my son has a severe ankle infection because I keep finding socks under his bed with a sticky residue on them. However, he refuses point-blank to go to the doctor, insisting there's nothing wrong with him.

I know this isn't a sports-related infection because he's a good boy who studies a lot and very rarely leaves his bedroom. I'm so worried – what can I do?

Mrs Quigley, Galliagh

Majella says

Don't worry, this is a natural thing for a teenage boy to be going through. Most young men his age suffer with ankle infec-

tions, sometimes as often as twice or three times a day.

My own boys are at the age where they are having problems with their ankles, and I find it's best to leave them to deal with the situation themselves. You are doing the right thing – just keep being supportive of your son and continue to buy multi-packs of socks (preferably white) to see him through these difficult times.

The frequency of the infections will ease as he gets older, most likely coinciding with him finding a girlfriend, but sadly some males never fully recover. In Derry, lots of grown men suffer all their lives from ankle infections, with most forced to take jobs as doormen and taxi men in later life, so it is possible to lead a perfectly abnormal life with these symptoms. Try not to worry too much, doll.

Majella

SWEDISH SUPERGROUP CONTINUE TOUR

Swedish pop super-group ASBO continue to make appearances in Derry, despite feedback from locals that their sound is now redundant.

The former chart toppers have made a string of appearances around the city in recent years, performing many of their classic hits such as 'Waterloo Street', 'Stupor Troopers', 'Owing me, Owing You' and 'Take a Chancer on Me'.

They have even secured a regular Saturday night slot outside a busy city centre nightclub, which is popular amongst Derry's gay and lesbian community. Witnesses report that the band has performed several renditions of their classic disco hit 'Dance on Queen' outside the venue, which includes a unique audience participation segment involving patrons leaving the club.

Seemingly none too keen on the song, however, locals are often heard to demand 'S.O.S' or 'Mamma Mia' during the performance.

A long overdue collaboration with The Police is now planned.

Derry City FC's janitor Kevin O'Hagan was injured yesterday when the club's trophy cabinet fell on him during routine cleaning, pinning him beneath several years worth of club silverware. Luckily, police were able to call on the services of John Terry, who turned up in a City replica shirt to successfully lift the cups off him.

In a further act of kindness, Mr Terry then carefully took the trophies across town to be repaired, with the help of a passing open-top bus driver.

Pure Derry

All you need is love. Cash would help too.

News shorts

Shock as female traveller collapses at City of Derry Airport. The woman, who has since regained consciousness, has vowed to never again to return to the city as she is still unsure about the correct location to have a stroke in Derry/Londonderry. Police are thought to be questioning a ham sandwich and a cup of coffee over allegations of suspect pricing.

John Hume spends day off rewinding people's old VHS tapes. Sitting with his thumb in a cassette before a queue of approximately eight thousand people he said, 'Most people can rewind it quicker with their VCR, but I'm always glad to help.'

Derry people were delighted to wake up today and discover that it was Saturday, after a long hard week which included a Monday, a Tuesday, a Wednesday, a Thursday and (according to reports) a Friday …

All except local actress, singer and international jetsetter Bronagh Gallagher, who is presently in Australia, where it's now Sunday.

'She was always ahead of everyone else at school,' said a former classmate.

NI PEOPLE 'TALKING BALLS' CLAIMS NEW RESEARCH

Ulster was depicted as a land of broken promises today, as figures uncovered by new research showed that people across the Province are continually saying things they don't really mean.

The report claims that in 2012, on over 250,000 separate occasions, conversations between local people resulted in a spontaneous declaration that both parties should 'grab a wee drink sometime' – without any subsequent purchasing and consumption of alcohol actually happening.

Similar verbal agreements, including, 'We must get a wee night out soon' and 'I must get a wee run down to see you sometime', also polled high in the findings – providing shocking new evidence that confirms people will say fucking anything to end an awkward conversation.

'I'm numb,' said John Dinnerplate, an IT manager from Belfast. 'I've been waiting patiently for my old school mate Mickey to

Aye, definitely, we must get out for a wee drink sometime...

text about that pint he always promises every time he ends our conversations. Now I'm supposed to believe he never really meant it? I feel cheated!'

The research, commissioned by the NI Smalltalk Ombudsman, also reveals that every single person working in full-time employment across Northern Ireland was either 'just working away, ye know', 'flat out' or 'ach, just keeping the head down' when engaged in conversation about what they were currently doing with their life by someone they hadn't seen in ages.

Taxi drivers, who formed one of the key sectors studied in the research, indicated that they 'sometimes wished they had their working hours tattooed on their forehead' to spare themselves hours pointlessly explaining their shift patterns to random strangers.

'I'm fucking sick of it!' moaned local cabbie Hashtag McLaughlin. 'Any time someone asks me when I'm working til or how busy I am, I just interrupt them and tell them about my divorce. As punishment like …'

'Why, what do you normally talk about?' our reporter asked.

'Well, I usually talk about my divorce, but I normally wait until they've finished speaking first.'

MASSIVE CHEQUES DRAW A BLANK

Editors at the local papers have gone into panic today, as an ongoing crisis in the financial world deepens even further. Due to recent strikes in the UK Printers Union, nationwide stocks of big massive cheques are at an all-time low.

Press journalists and photographers in Derry are now believed to be very nervous and frantically working on a series of back-up plans should the worst-case scenario become a reality. As a result, several local hacks are currently scouring the city in a bid to cover other monumental presentations and prizegiving ceremonies. A representative from McDonalds Staff Training Programme was unavailable for comment today, but it is widely believed that a press bidding war has already begun for exclusive photo rights to the ceremony of employees receiving gold stars in the disciplines of chicken nugget and Filet-o-Fish preparation.

Meanwhile, scores of Derry shop and office workers who didn't even want their photos taken in the first place, were left literally empty-handed this week, when big massive cheques could not be located for several newsworthy donations to charities that no one had ever heard of before. Quick-thinking journalists at the *Derry News* were not so easily put off, however, later reporting that they had improvised by writing 'IOU' notes on the back of rolls of old wallpaper.

Such is the panic at the *Journal*, though, that many journalists are believed to be offering large sums of money to buy massive cheques on the black market. At one donation presentation last week, at Muff Filling Station, a staff member reportedly witnessed a massive blank cheque being bought for almost £150. A subsequent photo of the donation, an £84 whip-round for the 'Greencastle Housewives Seaweed Preservation Society', later appeared in an edition of the paper.

'This article shows our commitment to bringing the stories that matter to the people that count,' said Prat McGart of the *Journal*. 'We leave no stone unturned in our quest to bring the Derry public the very best in local news! … Even when it's sometimes not worth the paper it's printed on,' he added.

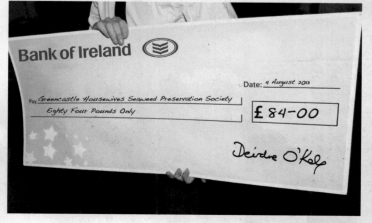

Bank of Ireland

Date: 4 August 2013

Pay Greencastle Housewives Seaweed Preservation Society

Eighty Four Pounds Only

£ 84-00

Deirdre O'Kelf

Other headlines

Derry businesses delighted as sales of cards, envelopes and chocolates quadruple in preparation for Valentine celebrations. Meanwhile, sales of porn, anti-depressants and low-grade alcohol increase tenfold.

Tawdry sex shop closed down following protests from parents. Local teenagers immediately begin going back to Mass, ironing their clothes and eating all their vegetables.

A Bogside girl off chocolate for Lent reassures boyfriend that she is allowed to eat chocolates bought for her on Valentine's Day. Later suggests he buys between ten and twelve boxes.

Sport

DERRY CRICKET TEAM CHALK UP STRAIGHT FORWARD WIN

The Derry cricket team chalked up an exciting win at Bumtoucher Field this weekend in a thrilling tie with Donemana Town which saw them progress to the semi-finals of the Cup a Soup Cup. Quarterback Peter Gordon was the star of the show, making a string of fingertip saves and some crucial touchdowns at key moments during the match.

Derry initially started slow, though, going four under par on the final furlong, and leaving themselves with lots of work to do in the second set. Thanks to some strong defending by Derry and a brilliant header off the line by Gordon on the tiebreaker, the home team managed to pull things back on the second wicket, to secure a 40-love lead on the eighteenth hole.

Holding a twenty-seven point average on the thirty-yard line with just minutes to go, Gordon screwed back on the middle wicket before hitting a perfect backhand volley to the touchline, leaving Derry 13 over and under not out, and putting the contest beyond their opponents … obviously.

Local fans were thrilled to wake up and discover they had won, celebrating wildly by going halfers on a celebratory cup of tea, before getting into their cars and immediately driving home, past several pubs.

Derry manager Percy McQuillan was delighted with the victory, saying, 'I'm proud of the lads, we played really well, but the searing heat made it almost impossible.'

Some of the lads were actually threatening to taking their jumpers off,' he added.

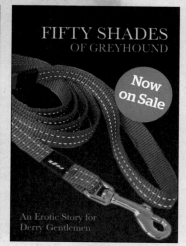
Majella's Valentine's Mailbag

Dear Majella

DERRY'S #1 AGONY AUNT

Dear Majella,
Due to overseas commitments, I'm unfortunately unable to be with my darling wife this Valentine's Day. I was hoping you could print something in *Pure Derry* so she knows how much I adore her, and that she's the most important thing in my life!!

Also, if you could let her know that the match in Madrid last night was amazing and that I'll be on the 10 p.m. Airporter bus into town – if she could pick me up that would be great.

Happy Valentine's, pet,
Shoelace McLaughlin

Dear Majella,
I thought I would write and tell you about my hunky boyfriend Mickey. He's tall, dark, handsome and always has a funny reply to everything. He likes to work out and takes care of himself, although he does enjoy a drink. He's got amazing green eyes and a lovely swarthy complexion. Basically, he's a babe!

Now that you know all about him, I wonder have you or anyone else seen him about? I haven't seen him for three days. Hate it when he goes on the rip! Let me know if you hear anything!

Love,
Spraytanya O'Hagan

Dear Majella,
My girlfriend and I recently emigrated to Canada from Derry, and whilst we have really been enjoying living here so far, the approach of Valentine's Day really makes me nervous. You see, I would like to take Donna out for a proper posh meal, but as far as I can tell, not one of the restaurants here serves garlic chips or chicken goujons! I like the place, don't get me wrong, but jeez it's so backward and unsophisticated at times!

Yours, hungrily,
Panfried McClintock

Dear Majella,
My girlfriend isn't speaking to me because I laughed at her suggestion that I should buy her some roses for Valentine's Day. I wasn't trying to be funny, but when I bought her roses at Christmas, she complained that she preferred Miniature Heroes and made me take them back to the shop and change them. I just don't understand women. Youse are all mad!!

Yours, confusedly,
Cottonbud McGlinchey

JOBS

CALL CENTRE INTERNATIONAL
WE HAVEN'T GONE TO INDIA ... YET

REQUIRE

CALL CENTRE OPERATORS

The ideal applicant will preferably be human or at least able to walk upright on two legs. You will ideally have absolutely no knowledge of computers and have used the phrase **'I don't even know how de switch dem on fir fucks sake'** on at least three separate occasions in the past twelve months. Full training will be given by people who only learned how **'di switch dem on'** recently. **Previous experience** is preferred, but people who can spell it will be considered.

Littlewoods   Waterloo Place; Derry

Require

Exterior Corner Alcohol Technicans

Due to liver related issues, we have several openings in the Exterior Hospitality Department of our Derry store.

Applicants must possess the ability to drink large quantities of Mundies wine and tap random passers-by for 20p. A stinking duffel coat and odd shoes are not essential but may be an advantage.

For an application form, please fall asleep at the store entrance and a member of staff will be right with you.

NORTH WEST CABS

Are Seeking

BANDIT TAXI DRIVERS

Due to expansion, North West Cabs are seeking a number of bandit drivers to cover various shifts in the Derry area.

The successful applicant must be well known to police, have at least nine points on their licence and be able to deliver carryouts at 5 a.m.

Perks include heading home when you feel like it, going AWOL during football matches and pretending to be related to passengers when the cops stop you.

NORTH WEST CABS

Are Seeking

Taxi Drivers / Weather Men

Due to further expansion, North West Cabs are seeking to fill a number of positions within the company. The successful applicant must be fully educated on all aspects of meteorology and be able to explain the effects of atmospheric pressure systems on incoming warm and cold fronts.

A clean driving licence, good knowledge of the local roads and a solid understanding of predictive climate change through analysis of cumulus, stratus, cirrus and nimbus cloud types is essential.

爱 THE DRAGON PALACE
'MAKING DRUNK PEOPLE FAT SINCE 1984'

Are Seeking

SERVICE ASSISTANTS

Due to yet another unforeseen pregnancy within our staff, we have a position available for a service assistant in our Derry store.

You should be able to write down incredibly complex orders with just three biro squiggles, smoke fags, fuck up telephone orders and understand Derry men after twelve pints of Harp – at the same time. Experience is not essential, but preference will be given to cheeky bastards. Apply in writing.

Sweet Nightclub

Bar Staff Wanted

Due to ongoing delayed hangovers amongst current staff, we are seeking to recruit several part-time personnel to help serve our classy and diversely aged clientele.

The suitable applicant should be able to memorise incredibly complex orders after being told once, yet be frustratingly useless at remembering the order in which people actually came to the bar. A penchant for serving your muckers ahead of others would also be preferred, but is not essential.

Duties will include: not knowing the ingredients for any cocktails more complicated than vodka & orange, short-changing drunk people and initialing the rota in the bogs after you've pretended to clean them.

MUCKERS BISTRO
Head Chef Required

Following the acrimonious departure of the last fucker, who had the audacity to leave and set up his own restaurant, we now require a new head chef to join our dynamic, winning team.

An excellent knowledge of world cuisine and the use of contemporary ingredients would be an advantage, but is not essential, as we'll mostly be using chicken, spuds, garlic, onions and mayonnaise.

The successful applicant must be able to make every dish on the menu look exactly the same, through the clever application of tobacco onions. Ability to make a wide range of delicious sauces and garnishes from mostly sugar and mayonnaise would also be an advantage. Preference will be given to those who correctly know that authentic chilli flavour comes from a jar of dry powder.

Zzzz-gate
Springtown, Derry

Production Operatives

Due to several boredom-related deaths, we are seeking to recruit new production operatives for our busy Springtown factory.

The successful applicant will ideally have 5+ years experience in occasionally pressing buttons, preferably from a standing position. Desire to have a crap social life due to strange working hours preferred, but not essential, as we don't really care, and you won't actually have a choice.

Duties will include wearing a spacesuit twelve hours a day, endlessly slagging off your workmates, setting up complex betting syndicates out of boredom and constantly trying to arrange shift swaps.

Own car an advantage, but applicants willing to spend half their wages taking taxis to/from work will also be considered.

Steever Bangle McHoop
Qualified Accountants

We are now looking for a suitably qualified accountant to join our busy city centre practice, which serves over 1,500 self-employed clients. The successful applicant must have experience of working with industrious, self-starting & honest individuals, who can often earn up to £6,000 per year working in various cash-in-hand enterprises around the city.

Experience in calculating income tax would be an advantage, but is not essential, as will likely not be required. However, ability to offset mortgage and loan repayments for lovely houses and cars in the balance sheet in a credible fashion is essential.

A flair for writing-off general household bills, Subway sandwich receipts and endless gallons of red diesel as plausible business expenses would also be a distinct advantage.

NI Transport
BUS DRIVERS NEEDED

Due to the large number of sick lines in our Derry depot, we require drivers to cover a variety of routes in the North West. Applicants must have a weird middle aged friend who gets on the bus for free and stands at front of bus at all times. Ability to talk to them while taking corners at 95 mph is essential.

Must be able to stop the bus inches from oncoming bus whilst holding up traffic behind and leaning out the window organising a fishing weekend. A first-class knowledge of betting forecasts and horse racing would be an advantage. A high tolerance to snowballs and stones may be necessary for some routes.

DO YOU HAVE A MUCKA?

WANTED

Car Park Technicians. We have a vacancy for a number of suitably qualified CPTs in our thriving Baghdad offices. The successful applicant should possess at least 30 years previous experience in converting fine old buildings into worthless mounds of rubble. A sound knowledge of TNT, Semtex and barraloads of fertiliser is a necessity and knowledge of detonators and timing devices will be considered an advantage.

Apply in the first instance to IRA (Iraqi Reconstruction Authority) 911 Bin Laden Street. Fallujah. Iraq.

BT
British Telecom – Derry Division

Require
PHONE BOX DURABILITY TESTERS

We have vacancies in our Galliagh and Shantallow teams for qualified destruction engineers to test the durability of our weekly-installed phone boxes.

Must have previous experience of GRAFFITI, ARSON and PUBLIC URINATION. Joyriders with two years relevant experience will be considered.

Uniform of Burberry baseball cap and half-price jewellers gold chain will be supplied.

DOORMEN WANTED

Must be loud, agressive and have unlikely-sized arms. An addiction to steroids a distinct advantage. Must be able to stare down anybody, ogle other people's women and punch fuck out of anyone smaller than yourself without giving any reason.

Short or no hair will be an advantage. Previous experience of overcrowding bars, handing out plastic glasses and standing on wooden boxes trying to look hard as fuck would be preferred.

Apply to : Bouncers Unlimited, Steroid Way, Uppercut House, Hospital Road, Coshquin.

DOCTOR NEEDED

In Claudy.

Mate just got glassed. Left eye's pretty bad and lip's cut too. Should probably bring some surgical spirit and gauze tape.

I really should get a mobile phone.

Derry City Barbers

Due to continued hair growth around the city, we are looking to expand the team at our busy city centre barbershop.

The successful applicant must be friendly and personable, with a keen interest in whether customers have gone anywhere on holiday, are up to anything tonight or what they work at themselves.

Ability to pretend to listen to what customer wants, before giving them the same haircut you give everyone else would be preferred, although applicants who actually pay attention may be considered provided they are willing to learn on the job.

Must be able to supply own equipment, including scissors, shears and one of those wee mirrors to show people the back of their head.

Pure Derry

The Vantastic Four

CAMERON TO RETHINK UNITED IRELAND STANCE FOLLOWING SAVAGE ATTACK ON VAN

Dissident republican factions have again struck fear into compact van owners around the city, after police found a Citroën Berlingo with its roof savagely hacked off by a Poundworld tin-opener on Sunday.

Two men, arrested at the scene, were yesterday charged at Derry Magistrates Court with being knuckle-dragging cretins, in front of a crowd of their cretin friends.

In further efforts to bring about a United Ireland, the crowd later tangled with police outside the courthouse, and cheered on the two men as they were taken away following their bail refusal.

'They were definitely the real deal!' said one passer-by. 'I consider myself Irish, but seeing those guys made even me question my national identity. The way they wear those Scottish football tops, and smoke them Spanish Lambert & Butler as they hurl abuse at police … God, such passion for the cause!'

In court, the van was described as being in 'a terrible state altogether' by one forensic expert, who claimed that the sharp edges on the roof could have 'cut the fingers off a wain, or worse, put someone's eye out!

'Oh and the stupid cunts left four mortar bombs in the back too,' he added.

On hearing the news, the DUP's Gregory Campbell immediately called for tightening of the laws permitting the sale of tin-openers. And vans. And Celtic tops.

News shorts

Panic spread across the city this week, following the BBC's announcement that tickets for the 2013 Radio One Big Weekend would only be available to households with a valid television licence. It is now widely expected that the BBC will receive around 55,000 applications from local people all claiming to live at the same address.

Snow Patrol's Gary Lightbody has apologised to local fans after it emerged that he failed to have his picture taken with every single person in Derry during the Sons & Daughters concert. The three people in question, who mistakenly joined the queue for a hotdog, were said to be 'gutted' not to have a smug celebrity photo to post on Facebook in the days after the highly successful music event.

A video montage of the best of Gary's meet-and-greet photos, set to Snow Patrol's hit single 'Run', is due to be posted on the band's website later today.

Sinn Féin councillor Tony Hassan has claimed that an eye-catching piece of public art on the Skeoge Roundabout will revolutionise the area. Mr Hassan was unaware of a Derry City Council internal memo proposing that the Skeoge Road be renamed the Galliagh Bypass at the time of his comments.

FOYLE BRIDGE CLOSURE CAUSES PANIC FOR LOCAL CHARITIES

Charities all over the North West went into a state of panic yesterday, when the City Council cut off their biggest source of funding by imposing an eleventh-hour emergency construction order on the Foyle Bridge.

The Roads Service has been forced to close the bridge for badly needed strengthening work, as the structure is beginning to weaken after years of unimaginative fundraising by local charities.

An estimated twenty-five thousand people per day have run across the 'two bridges' for thirty years, in a multitude of fun runs, sponsored hikes and wacky races, which engineers say have taken their toll on the bridge.

The bridge was opened in January 1984 by MEP John Hume who, until recent years, was leader of the SDLP. Unfortunately it has now become so weak and fragile that it could take years

of work to make it as strong as it once was. The bridge is also quite bad, say engineers, who didn't wish to discuss the SDLP.

Culmore residents welcomed the end of charity runs across the bridge, claiming that they had long been a problem in the area. A spokesperson for the Culmore Residents Association, Mrs Annie Price, said, 'We understand from what we saw in that film with Jimmy Nesbitt that not all areas in Derry have mansions but really, "Bogsiders" gawking at us isn't going to help the Foyle Hospice forever.'

Structural engineer and Culmore resident Mantlepiece

Devlin agrees that charity workers may well have done as much harm as good. 'Well, undoubtedly good work has been done over the years – many have crossed this hallowed bridge for noble causes such as Marie Curie Cancer Care and the Foyle Hospice. But, on the other hand, being unused to massive beautiful houses like what we have out here, visitors have increasingly tended to stray onto the western side of the bridge to gaze at the magnificence of our area and the resulting strain on that side has greatly affected the structure of the bridge overall.'

The strengthening, which will take over two years to complete, has run into a series of financial difficulties, forcing developers to consider the option of opening a secondary, stronger support structure to hold traffic during the construction work. Short of materials strong enough to build such a structure, the council has devised an alternative, and enlisted the help of the city's bouncers and cab drivers to create a human chain of bald heads, bomber jackets and steel-toed boots.

Since work began, fights on the bridge have subsequently been reduced by 25 per cent. However, hilarious comments about the ladies crossing it have risen by 4,765 per cent. The number of suicide attempts has remained unchanged, although many of those who have survived have reportedly been greatly cheered by the humorous remarks shouted by kindly cabbies and bouncers as they fell.

'I was understandably nervous,' says suicide attemptee, Dedalus Raphoe III, 'but they made everything so easy. One shouted, "Cheer up, it might never happen", and everyone on the bridge laughed. It really was the nicest bridge I've ever jumped off.'

Added Raphoe, 'And the houses there were lovely too.'

POLICE FEAR 'SUPER RA' HAVE GONE BACK TO THE DRAWING BOARD

Local police fear that dissident republicans could be planning another attack, after it emerged that a pound shop in Creggan had totally sold out of crayons and big-boy jotters.

Detectives are still looking for the workshop where a stolen van was modified recently, in an ambitious Hollywood-style plan to launch deadly mortar shells from a 'secret' hole in the roof.

Police are now appealing to locals who may have heard *The A-Team* theme music coming from a nearby garage in the last week, especially during periods of intense welding and angle-grinding, to come forward.

Capturing the rest of the dissidents is now a priority for the PSNI, although it has suffered a setback with a flaw in its criminal profiling of the group. 'Our profilers assumed they would love it when a plan comes together,' said PSNI Chief Inspector Bat Maggott. 'But apparently these boys love it even when a plan doesn't … so fucked if I know!'

Sport

DERRY CITY FC ENDS AGREEMENT WITH LOCAL TANNING SALON

The board of Derry City FC today faces increasing pressure from unhappy players following steps to cut overheads at the Brandywell.

The club has severed its relationship with local business The Tanning Rooms, which previously allowed players such as Eddie McCallion and Sean Friars unlimited access to Turbo Tanning equipment and exclusive moisturising products – all at the club's expense.

The cutback is likely to spark a dressing room revolt, with top players fearing their chances of securing a first team face are fading fast. It has already been reported that Friars' recent exit from the club was motivated by the removal of sunbed privileges, resulting in several Irish League

teams now competing for his services. An as yet unnamed club determined to take on Friars' services has reportedly offered him three hours a week in a top stand-up sunbed salon. However, a source close to the player revealed that he was likely to hold out for at least five.

The leaking of this news has already cast serious doubts on the move of Carlisle-based Derry-man Darren Kelly back to the Brandywell. His sunbed demands are thought to well exceed the current tanning structure at the club, though publicly the player maintains he doesn't use sunbeds and is half-Native American. Derry City remains confident that the deal is still very much on, but there are concerns from Coolkeeragh power station that Kelly's return will cause problems.

'We just can't handle that amount of activity on the BT48 power grid,' said a spokesperson. 'We personally hope that Derry opts for an African player. Or maybe someone with naturally swarthy skin.'

Dear Majella

DERRY'S #1 AGONY AUNT

Dear Majella,
I've been single now for a while and am really starting to get lonely. My friend suggested I should try 'speed dating' as it's supposed to be good. I'm afraid the rest of my friends will find out though. I'd be pure mortified. What should I do?
Regards,
Spraytanya O'Hagan

Majella says

Luv, I don't mean to put you on a downer, but I didn't like speed dating one bit!! Met a fella from Dove Gardens and he had a big bag of it … I didn't sleep for three days!!! Sex was great like, but jeez we talked shite, non-stop. I was like a bag of cats on Sunday when Dickhead dropped the wains back. I'd stick to the brandy and coke tbh.
Majella

CLASSIFIEDS

General classifieds

FOR SALE

Membership of Facebook Group 'Buy, Sell, Swap Derry/Londonderry'. Already own a TV stand, a two-slice toaster and a framed picture of Felix Healy, so no longer have use for it. Will consider swapping for a friend request from Pat Ramsey. No time wasters.

WANTED

Follow back on Twitter from local actress, singer and web developer Bronagh Gallagher. Have been bigging her up for ages but she continues to play hard to get. Please contact @PureDerry for details.

FOR SALE

Fashion sense of twenty-year-old Derry fella, complete with gaudy back prints, massive logos and stupid writing on most textile surfaces. Would suit thirty-year-old local man who looks forty due to years of drinking and smoking.

SENSE OF HUMOUR SOUGHT

Have been on that *Pure Derry* website and am wile offended by it — especially all the bits about religion, paedos, alcoholism and other morally offensive claptrap. All the stuff about the Orange Order is funny though. Please contact H.P. O'Crite at 71 933547

RECRUITS WANTED

Members needed to join local vigilante law-upholding republican organisation. Strong moral compass about all manner of crime and wrongdoing in our community would be preferred; however, fuckwits who left school in third year and can spell 'drugs' will be strongly considered.

COMPLAINER SEEKS EXCUSE

Ongoing positivity about 2013 City of Culture continues to make job difficult. Lack of activity by dissident republican groups not helping either. Please give instances of innocuous nationalist disturbances generously, for immediate point-scoring opportunities in the *Londonderry Journal*. Contact the DUP press office.

Property

HOUSE SWAP WANTED

Passionate Irish republican, disgusted by UK City of Culture status, seeks house swap to true Irish city where the virtues of a 32-county sovereignty still mean something. Glasgow preferred but Boston or Perth will be considered.

HOUSE FOR SALE

Amazing big house on Culmore Road with views over River Foyle. Two eagles on pillars in driveway, room for 3 BMWs and double-glazing throughout. Noticed it this morning out walking the dog. Must be worth a fortune! Does anyone know why they are selling it? Bet ye it's a divorce! Dying to hear all the bars! Call Majella on 71 934 777.

TENANTS REQUIRED

New occupants required for beautiful landmark building on the hill overlooking Belfast. Surrounding communities have had enough of the current tenants' constant bickering. Would suit professional types who are genuinely willing to share. Preference will be given to those with no previous history of blind evangelical faith, membership of hate-filled orders or leadership of paramilitary organisations.

Sport & recreation

BRANDYWELL SEASON TICKET WANTED

Lifelong local soccer fan seeks Brandywell season ticket. Willing to pay top money. Seat behind umpire or near sin bin preferred. Contact Mr S. Shine at 71 945555.

BRANDYWELL SEASON TICKET FOR SALE

Brandywell season ticket for sale. Seller unhappy with having to endure large crowds of newcomers at Brandywell lately who ruin the atmosphere and don't wear the shirt with true pride. Derry City FC has sold out!! Capitalism is killing local football. Will sell to the highest bidder. Phone Pat Boyle on 71 534345.

MEMORIES WANTED

Jealous Arsenal/Liverpool/United/Chelsea fan who never bothered following DCFC seeks hazy memories of supporting Derry City FC as a lad; the chill in the Brandywell during the '93 Cup Final, the feeling of Da hoisting him up on his shoulders in the jungle, sneaking through the turnstiles with his mates as a nipper, that sort of thing. Will exchange his entirely meaningless association with a team a good few hundred miles away that he only started supporting because they won something. So I've been to Old Trafford

or Anfield a couple of times, big fucking deal, I have led a wasted life. Contact every single fella you know on *all* their numbers.

MEMBERS NEEDED

For gruelling bootcamp exercise regime. Candidates must have multiple changes of expensive gym wear, ability to sweat buckets and a willingness to walk like Robocop for days on end due to overexertion. Desire to make continual Facebook updates about 'the new you' would be a distinct advantage. Classes start at 6 a.m. daily. Just £50 per week!

Dating

LADY SEEKS SOULMATE

Attractive thirty-something female in her mid-forties WLTM handsome, wealthy, funny, genuine, caring, loving

man with great body and amazing blue eyes, for deep meaningful romance and lasting long-term relationship. Are you 'the one'? Call 71 933697.

MAN SEEKS COMPANION

Handsome, funny, genuine, caring loving man with great body and amazing blue eyes WLTM beautiful, sweet and caring female with family values, a love of children and a winning personality for no-strings kinky fun. Must be able to drive too as my car is off the road at min. Call 71 555784.

SPECIAL FRIEND SOUGHT

Attractive lady, mid-forties — good job, nice house, own car — seeks loving, caring companion for long walks and cosy nights on the sofa. Terrier or Jack Russell preferred, but will consider pugs and shih-tzus. Text Mary on 07264465834

DEPENDABLE MAN NEEDED

Extremely attractive Derry women in her mid-thirties with two beautiful children, seeks trustworthy, genuine and handsome man with great prospects and stable income, to make scumbag ex-boyfriend jealous so he'll take me back. No time wasters. Call 07273749984.

Pure Derry

🍀 Happy Saint Paddy's Day 🍀

News shorts

Green has sensationally been banned from Belfast's St Patrick's Day parade in an attempt to offer a neutral and more inclusive celebration. Meanwhile, Translink Metro Limited begins legal proceedings against Belfast's gay community to prevent them monopolising the colour pink.

Shock as research scientists at Derry's Magee campus using the latest in 'Atlas Opening Technology' discover that Glasgow is in fact in a completely different country. Stena services across the River Lagan to the Belfast borough of 'Parkhead' now in crisis.

Normality is finally returning to Belfast following the St Patrick's Day riots. Loyalist protesters, sick of the four-month-long celebration of Irishness that occurs every year around 17 March, took to the streets to vent their anger that 'taigs are ripping the hole out of it'. Protestants are now reported to be looking forward to their single day of celebration at being British on 12 July.

SNAKE LABOUR EXPOSED IN DERRY

***Pure Derry* has today learnt that hundreds of immigrant snakes are being held in a secure facility at Derry Harbour until they can be deported to their native lands.**

The snakes, who travelled here illegally on several merchant vessels, are claiming Irish citizenship based on their ancestry. They insist that they have the right to return to the home of their forefathers, to work or claim unemployment benefit, just like their Irish ancestors.

Viper Campbell, a father of four whose entire family is being held at the facility, expressed his anger and sorrow at being treated so badly on his 'homecoming'. 'The Irish heritage of our people has never been forgotten,' said Campbell. 'As a young snake, my father would tell me stories of the great parties our ancestors used to have long before St Patrick arrived with his newfangled Christianity and started playing them fucking Tom Jones records all night. People think he threw us out – truth be told, we left.

'The green, green grass of home, me hole!' he added.

According to Campbell, 17 March was traditionally a pagan festival that was later bastardised by Patrick in an effort to ethnically cleanse the island. On this day in history, it was customary for tribes of native Irish men to wear Republic of Ireland or Celtic jerseys, congregate at villages and settlements across the country, drink masses of green tinted mead, and vomit all over each other.

Other long-lasting traditions, such as singing 'The Fields of Athenry' without knowing all the words, punching the fuck out of each other at the end of the night, and pishing on the side of police Land Rovers, are also derived from similar ancient traditions.

Several incidents of snake labour have been reported across the country, as opportunistic businessmen exploit snakes that have managed to make it into the country. This has led to angry locals losing their jobs at many of the city's twenty-four-hour petrol stations, as the hardworking snakes, despite not having any arms to use or holes to scratch, outperform their human colleagues.

Representatives for the FAI confirmed last night that several of the reptiles are taking part in trials for the Ireland football squad, as the team steps up its bid to find a long-term replacement for Roy Keane. Training sessions were cancelled last night, however, when it emerged that one of the team had been bitten and had later died in hospital.

Roy Keane was unavailable for comment and sources at Manchester United remain tight-lipped about the story.

'OPERATION HEROD' TO TACKLE ST PADDY'S DAY PROBLEMS

In the aftermath of what has been described as 'the biggest underage carryout session Derry has ever seen', the PSNI has decided to launch a last-ditch attempt to bring out-of-control youths into line.

'Basically, we have reached breaking-point and exhausted all other options,' claimed Constable Montgomery-Hamilton-Smith from Strand Road Barracks yesterday. 'As of 1 May all males and females under the age of sixteen will be rounded up and given the frowning of their lives by our officers at regular intervals in the Guildhall Square.' Constable Montgomery-Hamilton-Smith hopes this approach will set Derry's unruly youth on the straight and narrow.

'We named the venture "Herod" after the biblical figure King Herod who famously killed all children under the age of two in a bid to protect his crown from the Son of God,' stated the constable.

'We did consider a similar approach here in Derry, but permission was obviously needed from local parents for such a mass cull, and unfortunately the majority of those contacted were too drunk to give us any sort of feedback on the proposal. It was then decided that subjecting Derry youngsters to a severe frowning by the local constabulary would make them realise the chaos they are causing on the streets of the Maiden City, as well as instilling respect for their elders and private/public property, and all without the need for the bloodshed that King Herod had to resort to back in the olden days.'

SKY NEWS

LIVE   **PSNI Announce 'Operation Herod'**

Local community leaders have taken the unprecedented step of coming out in support of the PSNI initiative. 'The residents of this estate have basically had enough of these wains and their antics,' claimed Galliagh community leader Mickey Doherty from his home yesterday.

'I mean, they're bought scrambler bikes for Christmas, they're allowed at least three days a week off from school, and they never want for cheap fags! All we ask is that they babysit in the evenings so that us parents can fulfill our social obligations … and this is how they repay us. Sure even the dogs in the street are fed up to the back teeth of the climate of fear created by these wee shites.'

Mr Doherty's claim is backed up by what is now being treated as the first suspected case of animal suicide in the city after a dog residing in the Galliagh area of Derry hanged itself. It is thought that the actions of the desperate canine were induced by manic depression brought on by living in the Derry suburb.

'When the behaviour of this thug element affects even the dogs in the street, well then, things have really hit an all-time low,' Constable Montgomery-Hamilton-Smith went on to claim. 'It is hoped that once "Operation Herod" is under way both two-legged and four-legged residents of Derry will be able to enjoy St Paddy's Day without fear of drink-induced harassment or large patches of projectile vomit.'

PRAM CENTRE HITS OUT AT NEW LAW

Derry's world-famous Pram Centre could face bankruptcy if a proposed government ruling that will totally change the laws governing pram driving is passed.

Under the proposed law, prams would be classified by the DVLNI as 'Class C' vehicles, thus requiring that they be operated by persons over the age of sixteen with a valid licence. It is estimated that 87 per cent of Derry's pram owners will thus become ineligible to pilot the vehicles, unless accompanied by an adult.

As news of the law emerged late last night, Pram Centre shares dropped eighteen points on Derry's DOOTSIE index and the MOT centre braced itself for the fallout. A spokeswoman for the Derry Mothers' Association said, 'Hundreds of our members would have been out protesting last night in anger, but it was well past their bedtime.'

The fathers of the 687 children affected by the proposed law agreed to interviews with *Pure Derry*, but just as we went to press, both of them did a runner. Attempts to locate the pair ended without success when it was discovered that the North West snooker club was closed for renovations.

THE MADNESS OF FORT GEORGE

It has just been announced that the Department for Social Development has taken back control of the Fort George site from urban degenerate company ILEX.

Reports suggest that DSD officials were unimpressed with the ILEX strategy of building new civic amenities using Klingon cloaking technology, thus making them invisible to the naked eye.

City chiefs have now called in local actress, singer and starship captain Bronagh Gallagher, who will demolish the cleverly camouflaged infrastructure from space. 'She was always a cracking shot with a T4 laser cannon,' said George Lucas when we called him at his Skywalker ranch.

Potential new plans for the Fort George site have whipped armchair town planners into a frenzy of excitement. Ideas being discussed include a drive-through spray tan facility for open-top bus tours, a pound shop megastore you can see from space, and an all-you-can-eat Chinese buffet where you get your hair done while you eat.

Whatever new facilities end up there, it is hoped that planners will include a revolutionary free car park in which every parking space is directly outside the front door.

Other headlines

Irish heritage campaigners delighted as city street vendors begin selling small bundles of old-fashioned fresh shamrocks for £2.50. 'Tiocfaidh ár lá,' said a Sinn Féin spokesperson.

Shock as local fresh food supplier appears in court accused of overcharging restaurants for watercress. 'We shouldn't be paying any more than £3 for a carton,' said one disgruntled customer. 'It's a total disgrace,' added a Sinn Féin spokesperson.

Derry citizens congratulate Derry City Council for festively dyeing the River Foyle green for St Patrick's Day. 'Eh?' said a council spokesman.

Dear Majella

DERRY'S #1 AGONY AUNT

Dear Majella,

Now that I'm a famous footballer I should be used to rumours.

However, a new rumour has started to spread in Derry that I'm going to buy The Bogside Inn. Being from Creggan, this is something of an embarrassment to me obviously, cos of the local rivalry between the two areas. Me Da is already getting dirty looks up at the Telstar, and me Ma was asked three times in the town the other day if she was 'sneaking off' to live in the Bog!

I don't know how these stupid stories start spreading in Derry, but I wish people would stop or, at the very least, make up something about me buying somewhere in Creggan.

Regards,
James McBogginn –
Scunderland FC

Majella says

Ack, James luv, you can't beat a good Derry rumour. I think ye need to lighten up a bit. Remember the time that rumour spread that Tom Cruise was over in DFS in the Waterside, jumping up and down on sofas? Or that Morgan Freeman was filming *March of The Penguins 2* up the Diamond? Sure they keep the town ticking over and buzzing. Heard a cracker rumour the other day that Nadine Coyle had an atrocious Derry accent. LOL. I just don't know where people find the time to make this nonsense up!! As for The Bogside Inn story, I'll do me best through my page on *Pure Derry* to let people know the truth.

Everyone, Felix Healy is buying The Bogside Inn!! Ye heard it here first.

Majella

Pure Derry

Different horses for different main courses

POPE RESIGNS AMIDST THOROUGH-BREAD SCANDAL

Pope Benedict XVI stunned the world this morning when he announced he was retiring from his job as God's right-hand man.

The Vatican refused to be drawn on speculation regarding the circumstances, but it's believed that the ongoing controversy regarding the discovery of horse DNA in Holy Communion bread across Europe has taken its toll on the eighty-five-year-old pontiff.

Fresh allegations that many of the horses were abused have

since come to light, piling yet more misery on the Catholic church in Ireland. In shady activities spanning several decades, it's now believed that Epsom Derby winner Shergar (who was famously horsenapped in 1981) was eaten by the parish of Ballingar, County Offaly, over a three-month period at Sunday Mass.

The Pope, who is now entitled to high-rate Disability Living Allowance and a Translink Senior Travel Card, will officially step down at the end of the month. However, due to his failing health, the Vatican has confirmed that the step in question will be fitted with a ramp to assist him on the day.

God, who found the letter of resignation on his desk this morning, is now looking at applications from across the world for the prestigious position. Derry-born actress Roma Downey is on the shortlist, although insiders claim she may be over-qualified for the role. The *Touched by an Angel* star once famously missed out on a lucrative endorsement contract with Polo mints because she was 'too holy' for the brand image.

Meanwhile in Derry, many Catholics who were initially distraught at the loss of their spiritual leader, later went on to share Pope puns and jokes on Pure Derry's Facebook thread,

a site that many have described as 'a popeless cause'. The person who got the most likes was later believed to be delighted with themselves.

FUCK YOUR BUTCHER COUNTER ....
TESCO express
...I'VE A HORSE OUTSIDE!

DALAI LAMA VISITS DERRY

The world-renowned spiritual leader Tenzin Gyatso, the 14th Dalai Lama of Tibet, is visiting Derry today, a historic event that some local taxi drivers are describing as 'Ye wha?'

'Never heard of him,' said an excited Doledrop McLaughlin when we caught up with him in a queue of cars headed towards the Peace Bridge. 'But this fucking traffic is a nightmare,' he added before creeping 2.5 feet closer to meeting his idol.

Local politicians and celebrities are expected to be out in

force today to meet the great man on his historic visit. It has been reported that most of them have already looked him up on Wikipedia.

'Can't wait to meet Ghandi tomorrow,' exclaimed an ecstatic Mark H. Durkan on Facebook last night.

The details of the Dalai Lama's

visit are shrouded in mystery at the moment, but it is widely expected that after visiting the Peace Bridge today, he'll be chauffeured to Bap Express, where he'll learn all about our ancient traditions and culinary customs.

The Dalai Lama will then be whisked away to the back of Doc's Shop, where he'll join other delegates in smoking a 'single', before leading a spiritual pilgrimage up Lowry's Lane, where they'll share a bag of cans from a traditional blue bag.

The visit will culminate in a Children In The Crossfire talk at the Venue, which over 2,500 people are expected to attend.

'Looking forward to hearing Dalai Lama speech at the Venue,' commented Martin McGuinness on Twitter. 'Didn't realise they could fit that many people in upstairs at Rafters, though. Did they build an extension?' he asked before going off to decide what he'd order from the Two For £10 menu.

LOCAL HERO GALLAGHER KEEPS WATCH

Local singer, actress and electrical engineer Bronagh Gallagher has today played down her bravery after it emerged that she scaled the Guildhall to fix the broken clock lights over the weekend.

'I was just nipping out to the bank machine from Peadar's and realised I had forgotten my phone,' she laughed. 'Sure anyone needing to know the time would have done the same!'

The clock, which had previously been running two minutes and seven seconds slow, is now synced with the European atomic clock in CERN, Switzerland.

Sport

EARTH CELEBRATES MOMENTOUS GRAND NATIONAL ACHIEVEMENT

A momentous day today on the third planet from the sun, as the highly evolved 'human race' – renowned for its achievements in splitting atoms, space travel, microelectronics and genome mapping – prepares to watch dozens of dumb farm animals jump over hedges whilst screaming at their televisions.

To mark the occasion, special financial businesses have been set up, with the specific purpose of taking everyone's money and not giving it back to them.

On hearing this fantastic news, everyone rushed out excitedly to hand over their cash, along with names of horses they thought were randomly amusing.

Lambert Hegarty, who has been up since 5 a.m. this morning studying the form guide and betting patterns for forty horses and jockeys, eventually settled on a horse with a name similar to his first dog, whom he had dreamt about a week earlier.

Beanbag McCauley, a professional gambler who lives in an

opulent two-bedroom council house in town, was reported to have shouted at his wife for twenty minutes this morning, as he searched desperately for his lucky socks.

Witnesses later spotted him running out of the house to give the rest of his dole money to Paddy Power – as he helps them further expand their international business portfolio.

Women who never gamble are bracing themselves for being 'jammy bastards' when they inevitably win, whilst men who do likewise are busy preparing longwinded statements on their obvious skill and cunning for the pub later.

Next week, Neptune.

Dear Majella,
About six months ago I moved into a new house over here in Strathfoyle. Everything was going well until my neighbour came round and asked to use my phone because her own was broken. To my surprise she unplugged it, left, and took it to her own house. After an hour or so she came back, handed me the phone, and never even left so much as 50p.

Now I'm not one to start rumours, but knowing this one she probably phoned halfway round the world running my bill up sky high. Is there any way I can find out since my phone bill is not atomized?

Maggie MiWadi McCormac
Strathfoyle

Majella says

Well Maggie, as you probably know already, I am an expert with phones. In fact, Virgin Media and BT are always writing me letters about them. Anyway, it sounds like this woman is a menace and has to be stopped. I'd advise you

Dear Majella

DERRY'S #1 AGONY AUNT

to take immediate action and nip this in the bud before she starts taking the hand.

Next time she calls round, tell her that your phone only takes incoming calls now, and that you are waiting on an important phone call from the hospital. Tell her something outrageous, like your father went in for an emergency bypass after taking a heart attack in your very living room

only an hour before, but you saved the day by phoning an ambulance for him etc. This should put an end to all her lies and deceit.

On the subject of neighbours, I was talking to my sister the other day actually and she turned around and said to me that she was having problems with her neighbour. So I turned around and asked her why. She turned around and told me that her neighbour turned around to her one day in the garden and told her that she didn't like her kitchen tiles. So I turned around and told my sister that she should have turned right back around and said something. Apparently she'd turned around to the neighbour to say something when the neighbour turned back and said she was only joking, but my sister turned around to me and said she thinks it was a joke with a jag, so I turned around and told her that I never liked her neighbour anyway. Neighbours, eh!

Anyway, hope that helps.

Majella

BIRDMAN & BOOSTER SEAT

The Adventures of
BIRDMAN & BOOSTER SEAT
Pure Derry Plumbers

What do you mean you dumped her? She's a babe! I thought she was promising you the best sex of your life, any time you wanted it?

Aye but then I heard her on the phone to the bloody 'Family Planning' centre ... Fuckin psycho! I only met her last week and she already wants my babies! ... Her Loss!

Early Doors

Dude, we seriously need to find a new shop to visit before work in the morning!

This place is getting worse every day. I'm sick of turning up late for jobs.

Several Minutes Later ...

Two scratch cards and a lucky dip please!

Nutrition

So I said to her, 'Gis a Sausage Roll Bap please' and she was like ... 'Sorry, I'm all outta baps luv, do you want in two rounds of bread?'!!

Dude, that's disgusting.

I know, right?! As if anyone would ever eat something like that FFS!

Workin' Up The Country

That Dungiven job was tough. Your man John-Hames was busting our balls all day.

Which one was he? The site foreman?

No, that was James-John.

I thought he was called John-Francis?

Nah, that's his cousin the plasterer. His brother Francis-James was laying the flooring beside us ...

I'm Dungiven a fuck!

Drivin' Up The Country

Say what you want about working in Dungiven, but the scenery on the way back is stunning. Look at that!

Hear what you are saying, them big white windmills the farmers put in their fields look class, but I don't really agree with them. It's not right ...

??

Fecking recession on and them hoors are wasting electricity running them things. Must cost a bloody fortune!

Pedal To The Metal

Thank fuck you finally passed your driving test lad! ... Who ever heard of a plumber who can't drive!

Aye, it's sweet. Really getting the hang of the van now. Thought it would be harder to handle!

Good job buddy! Well done. Right, the van is washed now. Swap seats again ... We need to get to the next job.

Pure Derry

Don't Put All Your Taigs in One Basket

News shorts

The Harry Potter books have 'underlying messages that "subtly seduce" children' claimed head of the Catholic Church, Pope Emperor Palpatine XVI this week. The Pope, a well-known supporter of the ancient practice of 'religion', much prefers the more assured practice of blatantly programming children from birth.

Future world Lent festivities in doubt as archaeologists find the empty remains of two-thousand-year-old salt & vinegar crisp packets hidden in the Israeli desert. Jesus unavailable for comment.

Pope 'in excellent mental health' say Vatican doctors after recent health scare. Favourite dressing gown later made a saint.

A primary school wag who announced he'd given up homework for Lent was slapped today for being a twat. He has since decided to go off chocolate instead.

Jesus delivers Judgement Day press conference in Strand Road; 'Not to worry!' his only message to the Maiden City. Strabane later destroyed.

JESUS 'AWFULLY UPSET' AS LOCAL PUB SERVES BEER PAST MIDNIGHT

Heaven was in turmoil this morning following news that a local pub forgot to close early last night to mark the anniversary of Jesus' death almost two thousand years ago.

Jesus, who used to be human but is now an omnipotent celestial being who lives for eternity in an inter-dimensional utopia, is said to want strict adherence to the rule which prevents puny humans from buying alcohol on his big annual occasion. No, the other one.

Mr Christ, who hasn't been to earth in two millennia, is still adamant that he cares deeply about what mere mortals are up to down below, insisting that they 'get with the programme', or risk an eternity of fire and damnation in the pits of hell. However, he maintains he loves everyone just the same. So that's nice.

World governments have worked tirelessly for years to integrate religious beliefs into policy, in an effort to keep our traditions sacred and ensure that we properly respect our holy holidays. As such, pubs are expected to close early during Easter, so that people cannot buy any alcohol during an arbitrary one-and-a-half-hour window after 11 p.m., obviously.

'I don't go to church every week, but I believe you should have some sort of respect for God's will!' said local taxi driver Handbrake McCartney when we caught up with him buying cases of beer at Sainsbury's for the long Easter weekend. 'I actually think the early closing time is a nice tradition, ye get to spend more time with the wife.

WHAT WOULD JESUS BREW?

'Jesus fucking Christ,' he laughed suddenly. 'Talking about her indoors, nearly forgot about her wine. She'll crucify me if I come home empty-handed!'

It is not yet known whether any of the sales tax revenue from the estimated £175m chocolate Easter eggs sold this Easter in respect of Jesus' death will go towards repairing or building churches around the country, but apparently they taste really lovely, so that's Good News.

Easter Monday, a day of rest for Christians around the world, is the only day in the festive calendar that God doesn't require pubs to close early.

'All bets are off on Monday!' laughed St Peter when we caught a word with him doing the door at the gates of heaven in his Estate Services jacket. 'There are some cracking Easter Monday drinks promotions at pubs and clubs all over town. We're gonna party like its 1199!'

'Sorry luv, your name's not down, you're not coming in,' he continued to a lady in the queue before sending her to an eternity of torment and suffering.

CALLS FOR OFFENSIVE SHOP TO BE CLOSED

Angry Derry residents met with the City Council last week to seek the closure of an offensive shop, which is still legally trading in the city centre.

The store's owners insist they have done no wrong and are merely meeting a demand in the city for their alternative products. Those opposed to the shop, however, insist that it is a 'disgrace' and that its offensive wares should not be displayed or sold to residents of our city.

'I am sick of walking past that shop and seeing all manner of offensively carved and moulded shapes, some of which are up to 12 or 14 inches long,' said one angry group member. 'The pictures they have on display are deeply shocking too, depicting all manner of cruel sordid torture and debauchery. I have even heard tell that they encourage young women to purchase special "beads" which they claim heighten fulfillment. I don't know

how they are allowed to trade in this day and age, to be honest – they should be shut down!'

At the time of going to press the owners of the religious shop in question were unavailable for comment. However members of local anti-religion group Foyle Atheists, Infidels & Theology Haters, remain committed to the cause and appealed once again for the City Council to take action.

QUICK-THINKING KENNY EARNS DERRY A REPLAY

Derry United earned itself an Easter replay with Waterford, after some quick thinking by new manager Stephen Kenny avoided a probable defeat at the Brandykeg on Saturday past.

Derry were trailing Waterford 0–9 after only nineteen minutes, when a splendid hat-trick of hat-tricks by Waterford goalkeeper, Diego Eusebio Barthez, put the game beyond the reach of even the versatile and skilful Derry, whose combination of seventeen-year-olds and Peter Hutton so nearly clinched them their first 'non-loss' of whatever competition it was that Derry was playing in at the time.

Fearing that the game might be lost for his brave men in green, new man Kenny seized the moment and launched what has since gone down in Derry folklore as 'the turning off the floodlights' manoeuvre.

Not wanting to take any chances with common electrical sabotage, Kenny plugged in a toaster from Cash Incinerator – shop of broken homes and dreams – and took out a loaf of bread. Mother's Pride is suspected, but some reports say Irwins.

After a few dreadful minutes in which Waterford almost scored several times, Kenny's toaster gambit paid off and the inevitable happened. The Sandywell was instantly plunged into darkness and enveloped by the thick smell of delicious, cooked toast.

Fights broke out on the pitch initially, but were quickly quelled by Derry backroom staff, who told the crowd 'not to worry'. Taking his Handystripes team aside, Kenny asked them to muse

The amazing scenes at the Brandywell last night.

on the famous Siamese fighting fish and handed out freshly-made toast from the toaster. Waterford fans were said to be annoyed, most having travelled seven hours in the bus, and many having started out weeks earlier on foot, with their tops off and everything.

'My nipples could cut through glass,' complained one bearded Waterford yokel.

Kenny was uniformly praised by Derry's fans and team alike, all of whom noted his determination and poise, and his distinct lack of any panto involvement whatsoever. Players have the utmost respect for Kenny as a manager, and his tough, no-nonsense approach to all aspects of winning, as testified by his former players.

'I remember one time when we were on the way back home on the bus,' says Ronan Wideman, a quarterback at one of Kenny's old clubs. 'Mr Kenny ordered the driver to pull over and insisted that all of us jog home in the cold. He was really angry and said that it would teach us discipline and get us prepared for our next match.'

Added Wideman, 'That was the worst Christmas do ever! But then things finally started to pay off. The manager turned the team around that season – we were gutted when he left to go to Derby City.'

Londonderby's players, though, whilst happy with getting a second chance at the match, are keen to finish off a match inside eighty minutes like other teams, fearing they are getting a reputation. 'I mean, last week the opposing team were derailed in a car crash, the week before that it was killer bees, the week before that an anthrax scare. People are beginning to talk,' said football team person Gareth McGlynn.

Dear Majella

DERRY'S #1 AGONY AUNT

Dear Majella,
My problem is one that most men would no doubt love to have, and to be honest they'll likely think I am off my rocker. For quite some time now my missus has been badgering me to accept a proposal by our neighbours. A few weeks ago, while we were all enjoying a few beers at our house, they suggested that we should come around to their house some night for a wife swap session. I was quite drunk, and thought it was a joke, but the day after, my wife kept going on about it, and to my surprise it all appeared to be quite serious. The idea makes me feel very uncomfortable and I don't want to do it for a number of reasons.

Firstly, I love my wife. We took an oath the day we wed, and I think it goes against everything that our vows stand for. Secondly, I don't agree with it from a moral point of view. I believe that a man should be true to his oath and stand by his beloved til death do us part. Thirdly, I'm not sure I could live with myself afterwards. I'd feel depraved and abused and sinful.

Also I might add, my neighbour's wife is a fat ugly bastard. Every time I look at her my mind boggles as to how the poor fella gears himself up for doing it. He must have to tie a plank to his arse so he doesn't fall in.

Help me, Majella doll, you're my only hope.
Jobbie Wan Kerr Nobby

Majella says

I can't believe someone could be so heartless and shallow! Have you even considered your neighbours' feelings, not to mention your poor wife's? To be honest, I don't see the harm in it. I often head round to my neighbours' for a bit of *Wife Swap*, and the fun doesn't stop there.

When *Wife Swap* is over, we often flick the channels to watch some of the other great shows like *Secret Millionaire*, *I'm a Celebrity*, *How Clean is Your House* … God, the list is endless, and now that *Big Brother* has started again on Channel 5, there will be some serious orgies to be had round there.

You know, for all their faults, the Brits can make some great TV, and I think it would be a shame for you to deprive your wife of the orgasmic pleasure of watching it with another fanatic. I know your neighbour is a bit of a hefty lass, and so you are probably afraid to get stuck beside her on the sofa, but these are the chances we take for some pleasure. *Wife Swap* is one of the best shows on TV, so I suggest ye catch yourself on before it's too late and your missus starts looking elsewhere.

Majella

Pure Doire

Republican Action Against Something Or Other

FREE DERRY MUSEUM
NOW OPEN AT RATH-MOR

ADMISSION £2.00

TOUTS OUT

Republicans in Derry have just issued a warning to those involved in the illegal sale of One Big Weekend tickets.

Northern Ireland news

Fear strikes the unionist community over UK flags coming down. 'The journey towards a united Ireland government has already begun!' complained East Belfast local Robert Robertson.

Republic of Ireland news

Fear strikes the republican community over alcohol prices going up in Ireland. 'The journey towards a Northern Ireland off-licence will probably start next week!' moaned Dublin-born Paddy Patterson.

Other news

Change of heart strikes Antrim SDLP councillor Danny O'Connor, who yesterday suddenly decided to vote DUP. He gave no clues as to his mysterious political U-turn when we caught up with him stockpiling beer at Lidl. Speculation continues.

Dissident leaders were horrified to learn this morning that half of Derry had now become touts, leaving them with no choice but to issue death threats to those trying to flog spare passes for the Ebrington Square event.

'Republican Action Against Tickets', a quickly assembled task force set up to deal with the new influx of touts, was today hard at work burning cloakroom tickets of all colours, snatching bus receipts from scared pensioners and harassing people waiting for their number to be called out in Argos.

Staff at the Asylum Road jobs & benefits office were reported to be so scared about turning on their ticketing machines this afternoon that the order of seeing jobseekers was simply decided according to which one had the least money in their pocket.

In a further twist in this tale, the breakaway splinter group 'Republican Action Against

Tickets', a quickly assembled task force set up to deal with the new influx of touts, was today hard at work burning cloakroom tickets of all colours, snatching bus receipts from scared pensioners and harassing people waiting for their number to be called out in Argos.

Republicans' has since issued a death threat to people issuing death threats.

A republican vote on setting up further 'Republican Action Against Something' groups was today cancelled when the leadership realised they'd need to use tickets in their voting process.

After this morning's ticket disappointment, which left thousands of local people empty-handed after a farcical allocation process by BBC Radio One, an estimated 1,200 people logged onto SDLP councilor Pat Ramsey's page to complain that they didn't get tickets, whilst another 750 went onto Mark Patterson's page to complain that they couldn't get onto Pat Ramsey's page to complain.

Olly Murs, who had absolutely nothing to do with any of this, was reported still to be making shite music at the time the story broke.

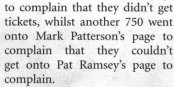

IRA STEPS UP WAR ON RUGS

The perils of leaving school in third year were painfully clear again last night, as members of the newly formed Financial IRA mistakenly went on an anti-narcotics rampage following a minor typo in a text message to operatives.

The group, which claims to be against all forms of illegal and harmful substances being traded on the streets of Derry (excluding gunpowder, Semtex and duty-free tobacco), shot and injured three known 'rug dealers' yesterday in attacks around the city.

One of the victims, who was spotted selling rugs door-to-door in Carnhill, was ruthlessly gunned down as he showed a sample of his Axminster double weave to kids outside the local secondary school.

Two other men, who worked at carpet showrooms in the Penny-burn and Crescent Link areas of the city, were fired upon as they opened up their respective stores early yesterday morning.

'Take that, ya rug-dealing bastard!' was the battle-cry of one of the balaclava-wearing drive-by terrorists, who then sped off to leave Crescent Link, only to join a long tailback of cars waiting patiently to exit the retail park.

In a stroke of luck for the assailants, police were slow to arrive to the scene, having responded to the other incidents, allowing the shooter's accomplice ample time to nip into the nearby Subway for a bite to eat before they made off.

Detectives have now narrowed their suspect list to local men with two eyes who like southwest sauce, extra jalapeños and hearty Italian bread.

Rug dealers across the city are now afraid to open their doors for business, leaving the public no choice but to buy cheap laminate flooring.

'They're just a bunch of fucking planks,' said one local man we stopped outside Maiden Wood. 'But this laminate flooring stuff, on the other hand, is pretty good value!'

News shorts

Republicans in Derry took another step towards a united Ireland last night after they shot two local men in the legs. The victims, patrons of the Telstar bar, who reportedly laughed at a harmless joke about Chucky O'Hagan's Ma, were taken to Ballymac and shot in the kneecaps.

'Tiocfaidh ár lá,' shouted a Super RA supporter upon hearing the news they had been shot.

'What the fuck did he just say about my Ma?' demanded an angry Chucky O'Hagan, before instructing the lads to bundle him into the van next.

Other headlines

RAAD issues statement denying prehistoric axehead found by archaeologists in Creggan dig belongs to them. Experts baffled.

Derry republicans grow increasingly suicidal at the prospect of Foyle Search and Rescue winning a Pride of Britain award.

IRAQ and IRAN natives suspected of leaving unfinished graffiti tags on buildings and toilet cubicles all over Derry.

Derry republican echoes feelings of the rest of city following re-emergence of tricolour painted kerbstones in the Bogside. 'Ach, it takes me back twenty years, so it does!'

YOUTHS NO LONGER SPELLING 'E'S ON STREET CORNERS

Ordinary Drry folk ar living in a stat of far, following last wks dissidnt shootings by th nwly formd trror group, th Financial IRA, or 'Supr RA', as locals now call thm.

Normal citizns ar now so afraid of bing targtd by rpublicans claiming to b anti-drugs champions, that thy hav stoppd using th fifth lttr of th alphabt whn writing – in cas thy mistaknly bcom targts of th dissidnts for bing drug dalrs.

This shocking nw dvlopmnt, that ss th loss of such an important vowl, is a major worry for th local churchs too, givn that astr Sunday falls this wknd. Kids across th city, who hav bn looking forward to njoying mountains of chocolat, ar now said to b disappointd that txting muckrs tlling thm how many 'astr ggs' thy got just isn't th sam.

Not all locals ar worrid by th dvlopmnt though. A Crggan man that *Pur Drry* txtd lat last night rplid saying, 'NAW MUCKS, I DON'T LIK DAT BUTTON NYWAY. NO SKIN OF MY KNOWS.'

It is also undrstood that locals ar also no longr comfortabl grassing up actual drug dalrs, using any form of pot, going anywhr high, buying cans of cok or going out for a bit of craic.

Furthr, th BBC rports that all of David Attnborough's wildlif documntaris containing any form of monky, hav had xtrmly poor viwing ratings in th Foyl rgion.

Rports on th ground suggst that th ovrwhlming majority of Drry citizns wish that th dissidnts would 'wis th bap' or 'gt a lif'.

Showbiz

IRISH SUPERGROUP 'THE IRA' TO REFORM

Following the unrivalled success of the Take That reunion, Irish supergroup The IRA have announced they are set to reform.

Several lacklustre solo projects followed the demise of the original IRA, including The RAAD, The Real IRA and The New IRA. Sadly supporters did not get behind the new material, complaining that they'd heard it all before.

Now though, all three groups plan to combine forces to make a new assault on the Irish market, in a new musical extravaganza that locals are calling the 'Super RA'.

'It's really a simple matter of combining our resources and focusing our efforts,' said an inside source.

The groups will now car-share a motability Ford Mondeo, and pool their DHSS housing benefits to get a sweet party gaff in an undisclosed location.

The new umbrella group will retain the original 'IRA' branding, but due to several organisational policy changes within musical republicanism, they will be formally referred to as the 'Integrated Racketeering Association'.

The Super Ra-nos

Republicanism, Redefined.

We tried to grab a word with one of their fans in a busy Derry street, but sadly no one owned up to actually liking them.

Dear Majella,
Although born in Derry I moved to the United States as a baby to live with my father in Illinois. I recently returned to Derry to live, and although I am really liking it, I don't know how to meet new people here. What do Derry people look for on a good night out?
Tiffany-Crystal Starspangle McCallion

Majella says

Welcome back home, doll, and I'm sorry to hear your father is not keeping well.

There are three main criteria for a good out in Derry. Firstly, the more overcrowded the bar, the better – there's nothing like that good old claustrophobic feeling to get your night rockin. If the air conditioning is turned off or broke then better still: sweaty fag-smoking bastards are an essential part of a great night, and if you are lucky enough to have an asthma attack, you'll get a free lift home.

Dear Majella

DERRY'S #1 AGONY AUNT

Secondly, only talk to people you already know. Everyone knows strangers are 'weird' anyway, so stay away. Remember to ask people the same questions that you asked them the week before, pretending to look interested when you realise you can't hear what they are saying. As a wee tip, just look at their facial expression when they finish speaking. If they are smiling just say 'Happy days!', but, if they are frowning or appear discontent, your response should be 'Bang out of order!' This has served me well for many years: I've always been told I am a great listener.

Last but not least, go for a pizza or Chinese to one of Derry's many overcrowded takeaways. On your way there, have the startling realisation that you are the type of person who tells it like it is. During your wait for food, feel proud of your new-found honesty, and convince yourself that everyone around you has benefited from your truthful observations on their wile-lookin shoes, apparent weight gain and bad dress sense. Ignore the fact that by morning you will realise you actually just have a tendency to be embarrassingly honest with people when you are drunk. That's what I do anyway!

Wishing you a full and happy social life.

Majella

DERRY ALBUM CHART

Occasionally at *Pure Derry* we give our readers an opportunity to hijack our pages. In April, we asked our readers to give the world of popular music a Derry makeover, and we received over eight hundred entries. A huge thank you to everyone for taking part in the pun-tastic proceedings. It's belter craic –with belly laughs and a few groans guaranteed. We couldn't include everyone's entry, sadly, but if you spot your work in the Top 40*, well done.

*Ok, so they are not actually in any order of preference. But hey, what fun is a Top 40 without a countdown?!

40. Paolos Nutini

39. Doleplay

38. Simply RAAD

37. Elton John Street

36. Fleetwood Ballymac

35. Will.i.am Street

34. McFlyover

33. Kylemore Minogue

32. Vanilla Ice Wharf

31. Lady Galliagh

30. Prod Stewart

29. The RAmones

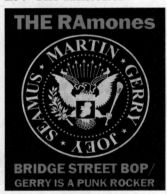

28. Little 10p Mix

27. Run-D.L.A.

26. The Monkeeyed

25. Damien Rice Bowl

24. The Prehenders

23. Our Kelly

22. A Flock of Seagates

21. Biffy Giro

20. Bru Fighters

19. The PRO-Claimers

18. Buncranarama

17. Johnny Cash Generator

16. P. Duddy

15. The Notorious B.O.G.

14. Tina Turnover

13. Doley Parton

12. City of Culture Club

11. Guns N Rosemount

10. Wile Raging Against The Machine

9. Emeli Sandino's

8. David Guetta Job

7. Cheryl Dole

6. Chris De Burgh Terrace

5. Apprentice Boyzone

4. The Aye Aye Aye's

3. Michael Up-The-Foyle-In-A Bublé

2. Taig David

1. Jesus Crisis Loan Superstar

Pure Derry

May the Fourth Be With You

POLICE ATTACK INNOCENT DERRY YOUTHS FOR NO REASON WHATSOEVER

The SDLP and Sinn Féin last night launched stinging attacks on the PSNI, following its recent use of CS gas against the innocent and friendly revellers of Waterloo Street.

Police arrived into the area on Friday night shortly after 2 a.m., following an altercation involving two young males was reported outside the swanky and illustrious Wicked Bar.

'It was nothing serious,' said Master Harpo McLaughlin Esquire, one of the men involved in the original incident. 'Myself and my good colleague, the polite and affable Reginald Jonty Meehan III, were just heatedly debating who would pay for the night's refreshments for ourselves and our lady companions. Obviously I was adamant that I should cover the expenses after having such a lovely evening, but Reginald is a stubborn old boy too, so he was very insistent also. We

created quite the storm in the teacup, but we didn't think that it merited the intervention of officers of the law.'

The incident soon spiralled out of control, however, and a fight broke out between the two

men just as the police arrived. On trying to resolve the dispute, the police officers found themselves under attack from a large group of young men who are normally so 'quiet and friendly' according to their mammys. 'Some of our officers were in extreme danger at this point,' said Hugh Dunnit of the PSNI. 'So the decision was made to bring the crowd to order using CS gas.'

The PSNI is now receiving heavy criticism from local nationalist politicians with nothing better to do, who slammed it for using what they described as 'an unnecessary level of brute force'. These accusations were rebutted by Officer Dunnit who said, 'We have had some financial problems, as reported in your paper last week, and this has forced us to ration our reserves of CS gas. Some officers have, therefore, been equipped with alternative aerosols, but none of them were using Brut Force – it was mostly Lynx Africa and Sure For Men.'

Officer Dunnit continued, 'We have considerable experience

in dealing with incidents of this nature, when a group of twenty or thirty young men get hot under the collar after a night of consuming alcohol. It's what's known among officers as the "24 Rower Drinks Effect". Its force is quite potent and not to be sniffed at – we consider these anti-anti-perspirant demonstrators to be quite dangerous.'

Maisie McCauley, a Derry mother of four, spoke to *Pure Derry* of her shock, anger, dismay, bewilderment, horror, terror, distress and lots of other words that she read in the *Journal* at her son's admittance to Altnagelvin following the disturbances. 'He was in a wile state when he got home. His face

was all swollen up and he could hardly see where he was going. It was just like any other Friday night, come to think of it, but he did smell lovely. I knew something was wrong when I looked outside and seen a crowd of girls' had followed him home.'

Altnagelvin was very short-staffed on Friday night, however, and a lack of ambulance cover meant many of the injured had to take taxis to the Waterside. Reports that a Derry taxi managed to get to through the Waterside with its windscreen intact were later dismissed. 'That's just ludicrous,' said Ronan Battle of the Kilfennan Volunteer Force. 'We definitely got all of them!'

Sinn Féin's Tony Hassan was

outraged at the shocking antics of the PSNI, claiming that there was too much CS gas used in Derry in comparison with anywhere else in the North West. 'I could understand it if the town was overrun by drunken underage scallies who are intent on starting fights with innocent passers-by, but given the angelic innocence and good nature of the youth who frequent our city centre I think it's a disgrace.'

Mr Hassan continued, 'The harmful effects of CS gas on the environment are also well known. We are therefore calling on all Derry citizens to stop dumping old fridges down the back of Galliagh as it's really affecting the ozone layer.'

OLYMPIC WEATHER FORECAST

Tomorrow: Expect frequent heavy downpours all week, with a fair-moderate chance of needing to phone and ask where the fuck your taxi is at least twice.

Thursday: Things set to improve slightly early on, with more drivers on call thanks to lack of decent Olympic football.

Friday: No chance – ladies beach volleyball is on. Organise a lift.

NEW CITYWIDE YOUTH BEHAVIOUR INITIATIVE LAUNCHED

The local council and the PSNI have teamed up in what they claim is 'the hardest crackdown on anti-social behaviour seen in Northern Ireland'.

The 'Naw Seriously Hi, Gon Wise Up' campaign was launched last week in a blaze of press coverage at the City Hotel, with officers and councillors alike claiming it will remove the 'bad elements' in our society once and for all.

Armed with a plethora of specialist knowledge and information, custodians of the campaign hope to show the youth of today 'the error of their ways' and encourage them to 'turn over a new leaf'.

Demonstrations given at the event showed officers in action

as they issued hard-hitting messages such as 'Drugs R 4 Mugs', 'It wasn't like that back in my day' and 'I know your Da, ya wee cunt!' Campaign organisers also revealed a new line of psychological questioning, which involves asking test subjects for sensitive informa-

tion such as 'Would yee do that in yer own house?' and 'What would yer Ma think if she seen you doing that?'

The campaign comes on the back of the successful, 'Fer God's Sake, Yees Need De Catch Yerselves On' initiative, which officers claim helped reduce

drug problems citywide. Drug peddling at school playgrounds around the town has been totally wiped, according to officers; a stark contrast to the dark days of a bygone era, when local colleges such as Grange Hill secondary school were plagued by these menacing criminals.

PROPERTY MARKET COMES TO THE CRUNCH

The property market in Derry reached new levels of hysteria last night when it emerged that a moderately sized cardboard box was sold for over £60,000 in Creggan.

The transaction took place on the premises of well-known Creggan retailer, Mr Johnny Hard Baps, at his esteemed breeze-block-dependent immobile mobile shop, situated in the 'Heights' area of the estate. Local housewife Mrs Dympna Splitends inadvertently began the frenzy, when she requested the handover of a single cardboard box from the renowned Derry retailer (famous for his ever-present stock of 'fresh baked goods').

Mr Hard Baps, one of Derry's finest business negotiators, was prepared to provide Mrs Splitends with the box, provided she agreed to purchase and rehouse the four packets of Tayto Cheese & Onion crisps still inhabiting its confines. The transaction was almost

finalised when well-known local estate agent, Mr Bonnie Crook – who had until then been parked outside counting his money and respectfully minding everyone else's business, entered the premises and sought to negotiate the sale on behalf of the store.

Mr Crook informed Mr Baps that the box he was selling was, in fact, a valuable piece of

residential property. Indicating the tangible features of such a box – cramped conditions, intense cold, susceptibility to damp, paper-thin walls and a large hole punched in the door – Mr Crook showed how it more than satisfied the local authorities criteria for living accommodation in Derry.

In an unprecedented sales pitch, Mr Crook pointed out that the box represented an ideal opportunity for first-time buyers to get a foot on the property ladder. 'Many homeless people would kill or maybe even work for such an extravagant home,' said Mr Crook. 'As would people living on the Lecky Road for that matter,' he added.

When the bidding for the property commenced, scenes of havoc not witnessed since the allocation of free EEC steak and butter ensued. A frantic auction was soon underway, and when bidding concluded, a young first-time buyer, Mr Ringpull McCafferty, was delighted to have secured his first home at a bargain price of £60,000.

'I almost made the mistake of buying a three-bedroom house in

Cornshell Fields for £70,000 last week,' he said. 'But I am delighted to get a bargain on a superior piece of property such as this.'

Mr Crook, having collected his £2,000 fee for estate agent services, in a final act of kindness which would have made Mother Teresa proud, offered to assist young Ringpull in obtaining £60,000 worth of crippling debt in exchange for a bargain £500 administration fee.

'I can't wait to get moved in.

Me and the missus were already down in Budget DIY looking at some dado rail. It's gonna be one classy gaff!' said Ringpull.

The Olympic Closing Ceremony ended in the early hours of this morning, after two weeks of TV coverage of the London event. The Olympics themselves, which also ran for about two weeks, have now ended too.

HOW A DERRY TAXI MAN FEELS...

...WHEN HE GETS A FARE TO THE WATERSIDE

Other headlines

Local unionists delighted as Ryanair restore twice daily London–Derry flights.

Confusion and chaos in Galliagh as Father's Day approaches.

NI Prison Service admits that Derry women make bad prison wardens. 'They never let anyone finish a sentence,' said a source.

Dear Majella

DERRY'S #1 AGONY AUNT

Dear Majella,
I recently went on holiday to Benidorm with my sister and her fiancé Joe from Ballymac. Whilst there, I met and fell in love with an amazing woman called Juanita. After the holiday we kept in touch and now she is coming over for my sister's wedding.

It's amazing to meet a great person like her. I've had a shady past – I've stolen cars, dealt drugs, burgled houses, mugged old ladies and carried out the odd hit and run. I really want to be honest with Juanita from the start, though, as I don't want to begin our relationship hiding dark secrets that I'm ashamed of. Please help me Majella. Should

I tell her that my brother-in-law is from Ballymac??
Paddy, Glenowen

Majella says

Well mucker, I'd start on your positive qualities. You've already said that you've had lots of cars in the past, and there's not a wee girl alive that doesn't love the thrill of riding shotgun with a badboy. The smell of burning rubber gets me every time. And the drive afterwards is nice too!

I'd say that by the time you've told her about the sixth wee Escort you nicked, she won't care if yer brother-in-law's from Galliagh, never mind Ballymac.
Majella

Pure Derry

Welcome to Summer. T-shirts Optional.

NEW SUNSCREEN INITIATIVE GETS BLISTERING RECEPTION

The Foyle Jobs and Benefits Office this morning announced their new 'Sunscreen Scheme' – aimed at helping the alarming number of local unemployed people who can't afford to buy T-shirts for warm days.

'We now suspect that many residents only have winter clothes in their wardrobe during these harsh economic times,' said DHSS spokeswoman Scribble O'Hallion. 'This leaves them no choice but to simply strip off when the temperature goes above 13°C – God love them!'

She went on to advise that DLA claimants can get free bottles of sun protection direct from their local DHSS office: factor 10 for lower rate, factor 20 for middle rate and factor 50 for higher rate.

Beyonce Quigley Hallmark Doherty, a higher rate claimant from the Linkin Park area of the city, said, 'Aye, it's happy days, cos my money goes in on a Wednesday and I'm pure lurd cos it's goin to be a scorcher! I'm heading straight to Topshop for a bikini, then to the off-licence.'

A local councillor said, 'We are fully expecting an influx of claim-ants to Brooke Park to bask in the sunshine until teatime, before parking themselves outside their houses for the remainder of the evening – wearing nothing but flip-flops, budgie smugglers and Primark sunglasses.'

The Foyle Benefits office confirmed this, saying that they had processed 3200+ crisis loan applications for emergency deck-chairs by 11 a.m. this morning.

The PSNI has since appealed to any neighbours who work and will be in their beds, sober, at a reasonable hour, not to be lousy and complain about the noise.

Summer weather forecast

Kitchen chairs continue to shift in an easterly direction across the Province as the sun makes its final descent towards the horizon.

A large cloud of barbecue smoke is expected to make its way west through the city shortly, causing nearby dogs to go buck fucking mad.

The temperature will drop later – except for those who thought that cooking oil was a good all-day moisturiser and who are forecast to wear no T-shirt until 4 a.m.

Expect to see some intermittent spells of pretentious-sunglasses-wearing late into the evening.

Tomorrow's forecast

Fucking lovely as well – pity you'll be dying in bed all day.

COLMCILLE FESTIVAL A SUCCESS DESPITE ADVERSE WEATHER CONDITIONS

Entirely straightforward and non-confusing marketing strategy for 'The Return of Colmcille' festival hailed as a 'complete success', as tens of thousands of local people flock into city despite organisers having to overcome the difficulties of three consecutive days of uninterrupted sunshine.

'I'm so proud of our wee town,' said absolutely everyone on Facebook, following the spectacular closing ceremony.

'I'm a bit gutted that it was only *The Book of Kells* in thon big secret box though,' commented Rollon O'Doherty on her page. 'There was a Derry rumour going around that Paolo's Pizza had cooked up a massive chicken box for the finale!' she added, before registering her disappointment using a 'sad face' cleverly constructed using a colon, a hyphen and a bracket.

Local taxi men, who collectively own the roads, were kind enough to allow the city centre to be closed for the evening, giving townspeople who haven't walked the length of themselves in years, the opportunity to walk the length of the town. 'It's been an amazing festival,' said local man Coolpix O'Hagan. 'I've never seen the town look so well – well, not since One Big Weekend at least. Or the Clipper Festival. Actually New Year's Eve was lovely too. Jesus, I can't decide!'

'Tell you what though, I've got some lovely pictures of the Peace Bridge at night. Do you want to see them?' he added before cycling through his photo gallery for two hours.

On hearing about the success of the event, Google and Facebook executives called an emergency joint meeting to discuss the best strategy for file and photo storage for the 2013 City of Culture. It is now widely expected that the two internet giants will open a 34-acre data centre in Houston, Texas, in an attempt to successfully archive the 347 billion photos of the peace bridge at night that are now circulating on the internet.

'Jeez, that's a lovely one of the Guildhall in the background with thon fireworks going off,' remarked Mark Zuckerberg in a morning status update to his twenty million fans. 'What's the craic with them big containers stacked outside the Custom House, though?' he added. 'Bet ye that's them Dungiven contractors again! Couldn't watch them boys with a bag of eyeballs.'

The population of Derry, who have been subjected to a horrendous amount of sunshine throughout the traumatic festival, are now reported to be suffering sunstroke, forcing many to take Monday off work as well.

'Jesus, I'm wile burnt,' said Spudpeel Delaney when he phoned in sick this morning. 'The aftersun and aloe vera aren't even helping, to be honest boss. But as soon as I drink thon pile of Carlsberg tins down a bit, there'll be room to stick them in the fridge at least! Should be grand for Wednesday!'

Other headlines

Ryanair confirms its record summer profits on its Mediterranean routes despite DHSS statistics that everyone had gone to visit their uncle in Manchester for two weeks.

Coldplay played to a packed Olympic arena last night, bringing an official end to two weeks of the world trying not to offend anyone by pretending to be interested in the Paralympics.

COLMCILLE ARRESTED

Saint Columba was arrested by the PSNI last night after leaving the Oak Grove Bar in Bishop Street.

He is being questioned by the Historical Enquiries team (HET) with regard to a battle in 561, which he is accused of starting over a book. Thousands of men died in the battle but Saint Columba says he was in Iona at the time.

His solicitor Paddy Mack said Saint Columba is a supporter of the peace process and has worked many miracles, such as healing people with diseases, expelling malignant spirits, subduing wild beasts, calming storms, and even returning the dead to life after a night in the Telstar bar.

Paddy Mack added that Saint Columba is also credited with Derry City's treble-winning season as well as the time the county beat Cork in the 1993 All-Ireland final. The saint denies helping Dana win the Eurovision Song Contest, saying that was an Act of God and not his fault.

"FREEZE SUCKA"

His solicitor said Saint Columba was 1,500 years old and had returned to Derry to visit his beloved Oak Grove, which he was shocked to learn had been turned into a pub. After he performed a few miracles, including turning watered-down lager into Coors Light, he left the bar for a fish supper and found himself being dragged into a Land Rover by the PSNI whom he described as being worse than the Picts.

Local MLAs said they would pray for Saint Columba at Mass on Sunday and light a few candles. However, one unionist politician in a statement said, 'that God should strip Columba of his sainthood and fling him into the fires of hell where he would remain for all eternity.'

Paddy Mack said that as St Columba's charges fell under the terms of the Good Friday Agreement, he would only have to spend two years in hell.

Sport

JOHN TERRY ANNOUNCES RETIREMENT FROM FOOTBALL

Following the retirement of several high-profile figures from the world of professional football, Chelsea captain John Terry, not be outdone, has announced his own retirement from the beautiful game.

However, unlike Paul Scholes, Jamie Carragher or Michael Owen, Terry intends to continue playing football for Chelsea for several further seasons following his retirement. He has confided in friends that he is now committed to retiring at the end of every campaign, before reporting back for pre-season training in July.

Terry was unavailable for comment on the issue today, as he was at Great Ormond Street Children's Hospital celebrating the opening of a brand new ward, in an area of the building that he'd previously made an appearance in.

Dear Majella

DERRY'S #1 AGONY AUNT

Dear Majella,
My wife has started putting on a bit of weight recently and, as a man, I find it hard to find a way to tell her about this. I love my wife dearly, but this is starting to interfere with our sex life as I don't fancy her as much any more. What is the best way to tell a lady something like this?
Seamus McCartax, Galliagh

Majella says
I think it's a disgrace that you are writing to me about this. You have to support your wife through thick and thin, even when it's not that thin. After all she has done for you, this is the thanks she gets? Buy her flowers and tell her how much you love her and accept her for what she is, you creep!!
Majella

Dear Majella,
My husband has started putting on a bit of weight recently and I find it hard to break the news to him without hurting his feelings. His beer belly is a wile turn off and it's really getting in the way of some decent nookie – literally. I've started comfort-eating to numb the pain. What can I do?
Leah McCartax, Galliagh

Majella says
Men are all the same, darling, useless bastards!! I bet he lies about the house all day playing PlayStation when you are out da town! If you want my advice, sack him before it gets out of hand and go get yourself a younger model down The Metro. Nip it in the bud now and get out of that marriage, doll. You'll get more money off the dole anyway when yous are separated.
Majella

RADIO ONE BIG

DAY ONE

SPOTTED: Rent-a-rapper will.i.am, in town to enjoy OBW, seen arguing with a traffic warden on John Street over the fact that he'd double parked whilst he nipped into Drinx for a c/o. 'Wise the bap, ballbag,' the former Black Eyed Peas frontman was reported to have screamed at the local redcoat. It's understood the two later patched up their differences and now plan to record a rock-rap collaboration track together, in aid of Mr i.am's favourite cause, Bigger Litter Trays for Oversized Cats.

APOLOGY: Dizzee Rascal has apologised to fans after one of his backing musicians mistakenly put the three notes of one of his 'songs' in the wrong sequence, unwittingly forming a melody. Despite the setback, the singer bravely carried on with his performance, whipping the crowd into a frenzy

with his acclaimed hit 'Bonkers'. Mr Rascal famously created the track by Sellotaping together discarded drum-loop samples he found in a bin at the back of Noel Edmonds's house.

WHOOPS: A red-faced Rolf Harris argued with BBCR1 organisers last night, after a mistaken double-booking saw him turn up to headline Friday night's OBW celebrations. It is understood that Mr Harris had, as instructed in the incorrectly-sent BBC email, prepared an entire set of dance pop hits including 'I Need Your Love', 'Sweet Nothing' and 'Bounce' – on his didgeridoo and wobble board. Despite the embarrassing setback, rapper will.i.am is apparently interested in the material for a new collaboration album.

JAW DROPPING: Dentists across the town have expressed concern at the alarming level of lower overbites in youth across

the town. One local orthodontist, who was watching OBW online last night, has urged everyone, especially rows 1–25 of last night's Calvin Harris concert to contact his surgery for a check-up immediately.

DAY TWO

DEAD SOUND: Classically-trained musicians The Saturdays enjoyed the famous Derry hospitality yesterday and, according to people at the concert, were 'actually dead sound'. The rest of the world, watching on TV and online, reportedly enjoyed watching them with their sound actually dead.

TAKE THON: Robbie Williams terrorised patrons at The White Horse Inn last night by turning up at the bar unannounced and hogging the karaoke machine. Manchester-born Williams, who wrote several successful songs many years ago during a

WEEKEND NEWSFEED

creative period when someone else wrote most of his songs for him, repeatedly sang his hit 'Let Me Entertain You' for two hours until staff had to ask him to leave for 'doing everyone's head in'.

SPOTTED: Bangor rockers 'Two Door Cinema Club' trying to use the wrong entrance at Brunswick Moviebowl.

SURPRISE: Festival-goers were caught off guard on day two of OBW, when millions of drops of water mysteriously started falling from the sky. Unprepared for this peculiar event, the likes of which Derry has never seen before, hundreds of ticket holders took to Facebook to complain about being 'wet'.

DAY THREE

COSY: Disappointed not to get any tickets for the last night, scores of local families settled down to watch the One Big Weekend finale by putting on their jammies and preparing to watch the event on TV. They then left the house and headed to The Gasyard, where the concert was broadcast live on the big screen.

SPOTTED: Bruno Mars nursing a hangover whilst ordering the mixed meat grill at Wetherspoons, The Diamond. According to sources he 'made a quare dig at it', but seemingly then became distressed by a sachet of sauce he'd fetched

from the sideboard, spending thirty minutes screaming at his entourage, 'Seriously, what the fuck flavour is Brown?'

DIE HARD: Derry people went back to their normal lives today, following weeks of intense stressing over One Big Weekend. The Northlands Rehab Centre has set up a special treatment room – aimed at weaning people off Facebook status updates about swapping tickets. 'It's helped me so much already,' said one patient we spoke to. 'I'm already down just to haggling for bus tickets.'

SICK NOTE: Following days of speculation that she was set to make a guest appearance at OBW, the inclusion of pop star Rihanna in the OBW line-up was dismissed as another vicious Derry rumour. However *Pure Derry* has learnt that the American singer and forehead model was in fact in Derry, but simply decided to phone in sick on the advice of her new manager Dorts McCafferty, whom she'd reportedly been partying with since Thursday in a flat in Carnhill. Her agent flatly denied the rumours, but went on to ask us where he could get 'a bag of monkey'.

Pure Derry

The sun is shining and the weather is sweet, to the beat.

HEAD-DO'ERS
HAIR SALON AND GOSSIP EMPORIUM

Share a Coke with **Yer Ma**

Other headlines

Millennium Forum unveils plans to triple profits by converting back to a car park.

Derry Iceland store gives up, starts selling skateboards.

Housing executive plan more Bogside houses to keep up with wall mural demands.

FIRST EVER 'POINT INN REUNION' ANNOUNCED

Following years of pressure by Derry citizens and support groups, local club promoters have finally given into the demands of the great unwashed, announcing that they will be soon be putting on the FIRST EVER 'Point Inn Reunion'.

The popular nightclub, which closed its doors generations ago during an outbreak of the bubonic plague, remains as popular as ever with nostalgia lovers, who maintain that the best nights of their lives were spent there.

'We had some amazing nights there!' said Kelly Housecoat from Creggan. 'One of our friends actually remembers. She used to tell us all the craic the morning after. God, I can't remember who that was now though... But Jesus aye, class times. Best nights of my life!'

The news of the reunion spread like wildfire across the city, as scores of excited former attendees of the infamous nightclub pestered their grandkids to send mobile phone telegram messages to their old pals about it.

'The buzz in here was electric when we found out,' said Martha Donnelly, an eighty-four-year-old resident at the Shanty Oaks Retirement Village. 'I double-dropped two arthritis tablets in celebration! I think I can feel them working their magic now. Will give it half an hour and then I might take another wee half,' she added.

Word soon went global, giving ex-pats living in the furthest reaches of the planet some serious pause for thought.

POINT INN
Reunion
Sunday 28th August

57

Old Skool House

Col Hamilton
Gleave Dobbin
Paul P

18+   **Strand Bar Complex - 10pm til Late**

'I've always said that I had no reason to come home again,' said Toecap McCrossan, head foreman on a construction site in New York City, 'especially since I've just started this great new job in construction! You don't get opportunities to lie to employers like this at home!' he added whilst figuring out to put his tool belt on.

'But one of the reasons I left Derry was because I was sick of local promoters constantly ignoring the demands of the people. For years we yearned for a nightlife experience based loosely on the popular yet controversial 1990s nightclub – The Point Inn.

Sadly it fell on deaf ears! Eventually, I just gave up and emigrated,' he added.

When the news broke, flights to Ireland sold out across the world instantly, greatly pleasing the organisers of The Gathering, a global initiative to reunite Ireland with its distant sons and daughters and their long lost wallets.

'We'd been ready to throw in the towel and concede that this idea might be an expensive failure that people had seen right through. But this 'Point Inn Reunion' has really saved us!' said Tom O'Rowe from Tourism Ireland. 'The truth is, the only people returning home this

year to Ireland had either been deported for pissing in the street or extradited for terrorism.'

In hindsight, rolling out the red carpet and trying to sell them Aran wool and Waterford crystal was probably a mistake,' he added.

Event organisers are now modestly billing the event as the one of the greatest spectacles the town has ever seen. The plan, according to promoters, is to bring together DJ talent who have never played together since the club closed – not even once – under the roof of one venue again, for an amazing night of pretending to be under the roof of another.

Former resident DJ Colin Bass, who himself now lives abroad, is rumoured to be excitedly flying home to play alongside his old partner, DJ Paul P, for the first time ever in over forty years. Mr P, now a successful Strand Road petrol station magnate, is reported to be setting up his 1s and 2s atop a hot food deli counter, where clubbers can request a tune with every hot panini, filled baguette or £20 of fuel.

'It's going to be banging!' said Mr P. 'The music I mean,' he added quickly. 'The food is lovely, as ever. Can I interest you in a coronation chicken sandwich?'

The PSNI is now so concerned about drugs being smuggled across the Derry–Donegal border, that they have now begun stopping bingo buses on the Buncrana Road, in an effort to train officers in the crafty evasive tactics deployed by middle-aged smugglers.

'We're on the lookout for the classic tell tale signs – chewing gum, Vicks, Fixodent denture cream, blue hair rinses … that sorta thing. These druggy bastards and their casual elasticated nylon trousers won't fool us!' he barked.

The first ever 'Point Inn Reunion' is on soon, somewhere in Derry that isn't actually the Point Inn. Buy now to get half-price concession tickets for the 2023 'Point Inn Reunion Reunion' somewhere else.

Music City balloon news

The PSNI has issued a stern warning to prank terrorism callers after receiving multiple reports of things being blown up across the city. The police, who are all still having a lie in after the G8, have asked Constable Lollipop Man and PC Traffic Warden to investigate further.

Local politicians are enjoying a well-deserved rest after this morning's 4 a.m. rise to help fill several large balloons with hot air. Gregory Campbell, who inflated two balloons simultaneously, one with each nostril, was only beaten in his amazing feat by local singer, actress and Guinness world record holder Bronagh Gallagher. Reports suggest she unwittingly inflated three after she let out a heavy sigh. 'She's so hot right now,' said a source.

Meanwhile terror group 'Republican Action Against Balloons' could be threatening

www.balloonflights.ie

to ruin today's festivities. This follows leaked MI5 satellite imagery, which shows a huge 'Super Pin' launcher being constructed in fields behind Creggan. It is believed that brief contact with even one of these pricks can deflate matters in seconds.

ILEX BOSS TO STEP DOWN

Derry urban regeneration company, the Institute for Lavish Expenses (ILEX), has announced that Chief Executive Aideen McGinley is to step down from her position.

This follows a wonderfully successful period for the company, with many staff becoming experts at making tea and with several reports of shoelaces being correctly tied.

ILEX are now on the hunt for McGinley's successor, with several candidates now shortlisted. Former Spurs boss Harry Redknapp is the bookies' favourite, with committee members believed to favour his growing reputation for ensuring sizeable investments go to the dogs.

It is hoped that whomever gets the job can replicate the success of public art installation 'Mute Meadow', which has been drawing in people, sometimes in pairs, to admire the incredible way in which it deceptively gives the illusion of dozens of rusty steel girders hammered into the ground at random.

Some well-documented technical difficulties with the art spectacle have now been overcome. ILEX have placed a sign outside the building demolition site at the bottom of Carlisle Road stating – 'THIS IS NOT MUTE MEADOW. PLEASE TURN LEFT & CROSS BRIDGE'.

Dear Majella,
I met a great girl recently. She's smart, funny, sexy and good craic. I tried to impress her by saying I went to the 'College', and rambled on about how important it was to get a good education and make something of your life, blah blah, blah. Ye know, pretending to be a wee stew.

Anyway, the other day she invited me round to her house to help her with her homework, and I near freaked out. I mean, homework, what the hell is all that about? I'm one of the lads, the main man like, and I don't do homework. I usually 'persuade' the wee stews to do that sorta crap for me.

Anyway, the only subject I want to study in your woman's house is 'biology', if ye know whadda mean, but I reckon she will not want to keep going out with me if she cops on that I'm simple.

I need your help Majella – what can I do? Should I keep lying to her or tell her the truth?
Regards,
Beltless McCloskey

Majella says

There's a few oul sayings that people use in situations like this, such as 'if this girl doesn't like you for who you are then she's not worth it' and 'just be yourself'. Sadly though, they are a pile of shite, and usually get toul by fat or ugly people who have never really lived in Derry.

See the truth is, mucker, this girl won't like you for who you are, cos it sounds to me like she's well outta your league. Being yourself simply won't work. My advice is to keep lying to her and hope that she doesn't cop on. Keep it simple. Don't be going round to her house and pretending to know all about Mathistics or whatever. You'll just get caught out and come out with something ridiculous like, 'the angle of the dangle is equal to the sag of the bag' – and then you're screwed. And not even in a good way.

Just tell her she'll never learn if you keep telling her the answers and pretend to read one of her other books. Yee never know, yee might get lucky and manage

Dear Majella

DERRY'S #1 AGONY AUNT

to jump her bones before she discovers the truth. And sure, at least then you will have something to tell your mates when it all eventually goes pear-shaped.

If you don't think you can pull off the lying act, then my advice is to give up on funny, intelligent, sexy women, cos you don't stand a chance. Instead, concentrate on the docile, easily lead, unattractive ones. At least that way, you can live up to your parents' expectations and be a daddy on your seventeenth birthday.
Majella

Pure Londonderry

The Twelfth Edition

News shorts

The Orange Order has tonight apologised to supporters across the Province as it admitted it is not able to deliver a huge consignment of leaflets to thank them for taking part in this year's Twelfth celebrations. Hundreds of boxes of the leaflets are stuck in a warehouse in east Belfast, unable to be distributed due to an unexplained Province-wide shortage of wooden shipping pallets. The PSNI has been called in to investigate.

Shock as Orange Order acts distinctly out of character, as band members are caught on camera wielding paramilitary flags. Speaking about the incident, Bogside Residents spokesman Donncha MacNiallais, who spelt his name specially for the occasion, said 'We were very surprised – usually they hand out Flumps and toffee apples'.

Chinese population of Portadown celebrate the beginning of their New Year with celebratory marching. Insist on marching solely through the most densely Japanese quarter of the town.

ULSTER CONFIRMED AS 37 PER CENT MORE BRITISH FOLLOWING AGGRESSIVE TWELFTH CELEBRATIONS

The union between Northern Ireland and Great Britain grew considerably stronger overnight, following forty-eight hours of peaceful aggressive Britishness by Ulster Protestants.

London this morning reported that the constitutional agreement between the two landmasses is now miraculously printed on an even thicker 120gsm paper and that the ink looks 'black as fuck'.

Across the Province, weird occurrences are being reported

to the Police Service of Northern Ireland at their new headquarters in Salford, Manchester. Old BT phone boxes are believed to be looking 'redder than the red hand of Ulster after slapping down uppity Fenians', whilst stocks of Marmite, PG Tips and HP Sauce are selling out fast at supermarkets.

'Keep Calm and Contact The British Consulate' was Martin McGuinness' appeal this morning to fretting republicans over his breakfast of a Ploughman's sandwich with lashings of Colman's mustard. But the words did nothing to quell the growing British surge, as dissident republicans met in secret to discuss the bowler hat shortage currently sweeping Creggan.

This swell of Britishness follows several successive years of triumphant Irishness, during which republican protestors have almost singlehandedly brought about a United Ireland, by scribbling out 'London' on signs

approaching the city and giving wile beatings to people who smoke cannabis.

It is believed the British government had been considering handing the expensive burden of Northern Ireland back this week, until economists reported that the Province's resupply order of wooden pallets and tyres would save the NHS.

Despite this opportunity to realise one of the Conservative Party's long-term goals, a Downing Street source said the PM had decided to keep NI anyway.

Other headlines

Sinn Féin delighted by unionist policy U-turn.

'No longer will we go down the republican road,' said Dr Paisley.

'We plan to go down every republican road we can find,' said Orange Order.

The Good Friday Agreement should be 'buried' claims Ian Paisley as he leaves Downing Street. 'You just cannot go back and do the same thing over and over again' said Mr Paisley as he prepared for the 198th annual Drumcree parade.

The Orange Order is said to be delighted at the return of this treasured painting to a Lodge in North Belfast.

The famous piece, thought lost forever, depicts William of Orange rounding up firewood in Rathcoole before leaving for the Battle of the Boyne, where he defeated over two thousand Catholic wooden shipping pallets loyal to the Vatican. Protestants still mark the event to this day.

Buckingham Pallets

ORANGE ORDER TO INVEST IN BUS

The Orange Order has confirmed today that, in response to continual pressure from its members, it will finally buy a bus for use in its parades. Its current mode of transport – walking en masse for hours with banners, flutes and drums – has drawn criticism from members who consider it 'needlessly complex and overly tiring'.

'On a march day,' says committed Orangeman Constance Walker, 'I'll get up as early as 5 a.m. to get myself ready and to sort out all the gear – the suit, the hat, the gloves, my sash. It's a nightmare. Then at around 9 a.m. I set off and, well, we walk and walk and walk for hours. It's very tiring, and really there's no point to it. I mean, I'm interested in the history of the battlegrounds and that, but do we have to cover it all by foot? And all these musicians and banners, are they really necessary? We're a historical society, for God's sake. Not an army.'

Walker's concerns are echoed by another committed Orangeman, Richard Peppers, who has for some time been trying to wrest the Order away from the needlessly protracted business of walking everywhere with as much fanfare as possible. 'Take the route of the Twelfth. It takes us hours and we're blocking main roads and causing quite a bit of disturbance with all those bands and that. I mean, nobody's complained, but really I wouldn't like to think that my hobby was putting anybody out.'

'And that's exactly it,' says Walker. 'I mean I read the other day that some Catholics weren't best pleased with the whole thing and I suddenly thought – God! We're kind of … in a way, what we're doing is celebrating their ancestors' deaths! And, I mean, that's not how we meant it at all!'

'No,' says Peppers, 'not at all! We were shocked and appalled to hear that some Catholics felt that way, and in the end it was that revelation which led to the council unanimously passing the resolution to buy the bus. God, we just felt terrible about the whole thing.'

But foremost in their minds was the exertion required of marchers to get from route to route. Says Peppers, 'Many of our members are quite old and walking is just not feasible for them, especially not for six or seven hours on the hottest day of the year! So we can pack ourselves into a big bus for about forty-five minutes, air conditioning on, and just drive through every route we want to and talk about the history in a relaxed atmosphere.'

'And the best part,' says Walker, 'is we can stick on some music and save ourselves the bother of packing all those drums and flutes. And play any music we like as well! I know I shouldn't really be saying this, but I'm not the biggest fan of that kind of music anyway. I'm more of an ABBA man myself.'

Some people have criticised the move, claiming it to be an affront to the tradition of truly recreating King William's marching on foot to battle.

Peppers dismisses this. 'Bollocks,' he says. 'I don't think King Billy ever wore a bowler hat, and he certainly didn't have a black brolly. We are a historical society dedicated to commemorating some moments from our past. We'd much rather be reading old texts from battle in our local libraries, excavating battle sites or making period costumes than causing trouble. It's not rocket science. Why should our penchant for history bother those who consider the bitter and violent war over this land an abomination?'

NEXT YEAR'S TWELFTH IN JEOPARDY

Researchers at Magee University, in a shocking new doomsday scenario, have predicted that that large swathes of the country will be submerged under two hundred feet of water by this time next year.

Their research has produced the first detailed maps of the possible catastrophe, showing the true impact of global warming on marching season. The absolute worst-case scenario, should the entire Antarctic ice sheet melt, is that much of the Province will vanish. Naturally, this will put the annual Twelfth celebrations in considerable jeopardy.

Professor Tushima Tsunami said, 'Our research suggests that the entire Foyle Basin will succumb within the next twelve months. The only Derry people likely to survive will be those living in areas more than two-hundred feet above sea level. Craigavon Bridge will be no more, and the same goes for Carlisle Road, the Diamond and Bishop Street.

'It is our belief that Orangemen will have to rethink their planned route for next year and, if they are going to have a parade at all, it will have to be held in either Gobnascale or Creggan, as those areas will be the only surviving parts of the city. It's as simple as that.'

The self-appointed head of the Bogside Residents Group, Deborah O'Zebra, said, 'We have been in contact with the Parades Commission regarding the plans for next year and informed them, in no uncertain terms, that in the event of the expected deluge, I will be the leader of the Creggan Residents Group and that the Orange Order will have to talk to me if they want to march through Creggan.'

Members of the Independent Orange Order, led by the Reverend Ian Paisley, say they are 'unfazed' by the predictions of impending doom. The Grand Cyclops of the Order, Cedric Burntaigs, said, 'This situation is of no concern to us. Sure we all know that Free Presbyterians can walk on water. It is written in the Good Book.'

Chief Superintendent Wesley Watters of the PSNI Sub-Aqua Division said, 'We don't expect the rising water levels to pose any operational difficulties for us. Our men will be on duty in their high visibility scuba-diver riot fatigues and they will be able to handle all eventualities. In fact we are currently redeveloping our plastic bullets for underwater use. All future plastic bullets will come complete with a dorsal fin.'

FIVE MORE CARS THAT UNIONISTS DIDN'T WANT THE WORLD TO HAVE

Following the DUP's well-documented meltdown about the proposed new Kia 'Provo' concept car, we look back at five other car projects which failed after complaints from Northern Ireland unionists.

1996 – THE BMW .32 COUNTY SERIES

The usually efficient Germans made a balls of branding their new rural saloon line and found themselves getting death threats from Mad Dog Johnny Adair. He later tried to order one just so he could key it and smash the headlights in with a hammer.

1998 – THE FORD CEMTEX

This nippy family car was due to roll off the production line in June 1998 until Big Ian Paisley kicked up a fuss in the House of Commons. It was later rebranded and released as the Focus, but unionists never forgot, which explains the statistically poor sales of this otherwise popular model in East Belfast, especially in green.

2002 – THE PEUGEOT PUNISHMENT BEATING

This risqué choice for the French car makers landed them in hot water with NI politicians. The

design of this otherwise unassuming large saloon car had blacked-out windows, spacious back seats and removable Velcro numberplates. Gregory Campbell actually busted a blood vessel in his temple whilst on the phone complaining to Peugeot.

2007 – THE VAUXHALL C'MON THE HOOPS

Originally planned as a fun, about-town vehicle for young professionals, this controversial car was scrapped after the DUP complained to the UK National Consumer Council. The prototype was reportedly stolen by joyriders and found burnt out in Creggan.

2013 – THE LAMBORGHINI TAIG

Staff at the classy Italian sports car manufacturer were shocked to find 350 fleg protestors picketing their headquarters at Bolognese, Italy, after announcing this new car – forcing them to scrap £100 million worth of R&D on the project. The DUP has never forgiven them, though, advising members to avoid buying Diablos & Gallardos in favour of executive Skoda Octavias or Volvos.

Breaking news

Dissident republicans in Creggan, not to be outdone by their neighbours' planned Eleventh Night celebrations, have just constructed a massive magnifying glass at the back of the 'Heights'.

It is hoped the new structure will allow them to direct today's baking sunlight onto distant bonfires, in an effort to spoil proceedings by setting them alight ahead of schedule.

Local women are also believed to be queuing up at the site, as dissident factions have prom-ised to 'super charge' their tans for £3.50 – provided they don't have any drugs in their handbags and can show sufficient evidence that they haven't paid their TV licences.

The PSNI have confirmed that they are looking into it.

Dear Majella

DERRY'S #1 AGONY AUNT

Dear Majella,
I am very disturbed today by the sheer lunacy and hypocrisy witnessed at the recent TV coverage of the big wedding. I think that by getting married again, he has taken a massive gamble with his reputation. A man of his position and stature should know better than to allow such a woman to cloud his judgment. Don't you agree?

The first wedding in 1981 was a joyous occasion, and I was delighted to see such beautiful coronation scenes, but the recent event left a bad taste in my mouth, and I couldn't help but feel that he has made a massive mistake in the eyes of his adoring public. In light of the well documented allegations of adultery which preceded their wedding, and since they are both divorcees, I think that they have run the risk of losing the support of the community.

I was wondering what your feelings were on this, and if you have any advice for someone like me who has been so deeply affected by the horrendous affair.

Yours,
Ms Lilac Hatpin-Anklesocks

Majella says

Ye know what, I totally agree. When Ken married Deirdre the first time, I was over the moon. She was a lovely girl back then, but ever since she had her wicked way with oul Mike Baldwin, we stopped trusting her. (Our Kathy hates her guts.) As me Ma would always say, though, 'Once a cheater always a cheater', and she was proved right.

In saying that, it's not like he has always been an angel, but his heart is in the right place sure. I agree that he has taken a gamble with his reputation, what with him being the headmaster of the school and all, but I reckon she is the one to watch out for.

Do you remember sure she was tarting about with that Indian fella a few years ago sure? Aye! … and sure we all know what happened to him!! Our Teresa reckons she was involved somehow, but sure we'll probably never find out if there's any truth in that now.

I dunno, it's amazing what them people get away with just cos they are on TV.

Listen, love, if you want my advice, don't take it too much to heart. Sure there are always plenty of other documentaries like *Emmerdale*, *Home & Away* and *Hollyoaks* to keep your mind occupied when you're bringing up your wains.

Hope this helps.

Majella

Pure Derry

Summer loving, had me a blast. (Still a bit stoned, tbh!)

News shorts

Galliagh youths are extremely angry that local authorities removed bonfire materials from Moss Park. 'By hook or by crook, we'll be burning lots of dead wood this summer!' said Reebok McCarron. The PSNI has placed extra security at the City Council offices on the Strand Road as a precaution.

Randy criminals strike as local sex shop is burgled. Over one hundred sex toys were stolen by a gang of kleptomaniac nymphomaniacs from Cupid's Corner on Waterloo Street yesterday. The PSNI have since admitted that thefts of sex toys in the area are rampant.

Residents of Galliagh, distraught at the council's clampdown on the 15 August bonfire, have been given a special helpline number to help them through this difficult period – just call 02871 222 777 for advice and support.

This news bulletin has been sponsored by PRO SKIP HIRE. Telephone 02871 222 777.

FIELD OF DREAMS

Derry's teenagers and underage drinking population have hit out at the lack of decent loitering facilities in the city. The criticism comes after a local woman and her husband reported witnessing two teenagers having sex in the field at around 8.30 p.m. on Saturday night.

'I was just disgusted,' the woman said. 'My husband had been upstairs in our house when he suddenly came running down saying that he was going out to get the wain who was playing in the field.'

It was later suggested that her husband was in fact going to get his camcorder so he could record the incident.

Spotrick McAcne, a spokesperson for the underage drinking campaign group 'Swear Ma, We're Just Goin De The Bowlin Alley', contacted *Pure Derry* to speak of his outrage at the news. 'Who do these people think they are?' he said. 'We work hard all week at school and come the weekend we like to relax a little. As far as I can see, we aren't doing anything wrong. My big brother goes out every weekend and gets drunk and gets a ride – and you don't read about him in the paper!

'Unless you count them pictures of him down at the Bimbo Beach Club in the *Derry News*, or at the wain's christening in the *Journal*. Oh aye, and them photos from the riot last week.'

Since the revelation that adults have been perving on hedonistic teenagers in Lowry's Lane, *Pure Derry* has been swamped with complaints from teens all over the city about the lack of decent drinking facilities or privacy in the city nowadays.

Unfortunate redevelopments and investments have seen many of the city's drinking landmarks disappear, including the Foyle Street Bandstand, the Bay Road, the Foyle Arts Centre, the Creggan Rez and the Collon Lane.

'There's just nowhere decent to go and get hammered anymore,' said fifteen-year-old Gelflick McDaid. 'Me Ma is always going on about the great times she used to have drinking up the Creggan Rez and how she first met me Da up there. She loves telling that story.

'She swears she's gonna remember his name one of these days too!' he laughed.

Aside from the rapidly vanishing drinking spots in town, the surge of cheap drink at multinational pubs is hitting Derry hard. Sales at local off-licences across the city have dropped drastically, causing stocks in the P.J. Bargainbooze empire to drop six points on the DOOTSIE index in recent weeks.

'The wains have started heading to the pubs now instead,' said Hiccup McCarron of Quare Value. 'Lowry's Lane is one of the last remaining bastions for teenage debauchery in Derry, and pretty soon that'll be lost to redevelopment. We will have no customers left except the taps and drunks who stand at the corner,' he lamented. 'Please give generously.'

The field at the centre of this storm is in the middle of another ongoing row in the community, which is causing arguments between angry residents. The field is being considered for use as a GAA facility, which will see the entire surface being fenced off and used exclusively by big fellas from up the country. Buck McTuskan, a concerned local, is disgusted by the plans, claiming it will take away the only decent local amenity for kids in the area.

'Where will they go to fly their kites now?' he demanded.

COLD AGE PENSIONERS

Following the news that residential care homes across the Province are set to shut, Stormont chiefs have announced plans to keep pensioners warm in their homes this winter by burning other pensioners.

Local councils have been instructed to install 'Granny Collection Banks' at their recycling centres, where families can deposit any useless old family members who are no longer paying taxes.

'Just one bingo bus of elderly people could heat an entire housing estate for a month!' said one ecstatic MLA.

'Or all the care homes in the Northern Health Trust until the end of time,' he joked.

If you know an old person who has stopped being relevant to HMRC, please call your local sanitation department immediately. Please note that old sofas, leaky fridges and disused washing machines cannot be collected by this service – unless accompanied by a pensioner.

Fermanagh G8 summit: news compendium

A new chapter in Northern Ireland's history began today when the Province's roads came to a complete standstill over something to do with politics.

'What's the craic?' asks President Obama whilst addressing the crowd in the Odyssey Arena. 'Fuck all, big lad, yerself? Ye taking her handy?' responds man twenty-seven rows from front. Sadly mic doesn't pick up the audio.

Every single police officer in NI posted in Fermanagh, leaving local PSNI stations to be manned by alternates and temps. 'I assure you that we have the situation under control,' said Chief Inspector Mr Whippy during an emergency callout to a double homicide in Galliagh.

History is made as world leaders finally descend on Fermanagh for G8 summit. Syria immediately made top of agenda. 'Where the hell is that?' asks clueless Derryman on Mark H. Durkan's Facebook page. 'LOL,' replied the SDLP whizz. 'Fermanagh's in Tyrone, ya madman!!'

Whole of country reassured that rest of world still loves us, that we have a great sense of humour and that our scenery is beautiful. Later decide to still get every local reporter to ask every attendee anyway – just to be sure.

REUTERS report that Russian president Vladimir Putin is so scandalised at the price of a measure of vodka in the luxurious Fermanagh Golf Resort, that he sent two KGB operatives to Tesco in Enniskillen. He reportedly spent the rest of the day pouring measures of Smirnoff under the table, fuelling speculation that he may be planning to get married in Ireland.

US Presidude Barack Obama has been lambasted as a hypocrite by American conservatives, after a Father's Day picture showed him having a water pistol fight with his kids. Conspiracy theorists have now postulated that Hawaiian-born Obama may have a secret agenda to some day gain control of the largest military force in the world, giving him full control of millions of *actual* guns.

The worlds of fashion and politics collided at full speed, as the G8's new 'smart casual' approach was publically supported by

David Cameron and George Osborne, who both attended the event without jacket or tie. The move was also introduced locally by Sinn Féin members, who all turned up at regional offices today wearing tracksuits and trainers. 'Eh?' replied Martin McGuinness when we asked him about the party's support for the new casual dress code.

Tax avoidance was high on the agenda for world leaders as governments sought a solution for multinational corporations who continue to take taxpayers' money without actually paying tax on it. 'Going halfers' is believed to have been an early suggestion by Chancellor George Osborne. Facebook later went into an ironic meltdown, as thousands of unemployed people took to the internet to complain about how much taxpayers' money was wasted policing the Fermanagh event.

Fashion news

Following the row surrounding his attendance at an official Derry City Council meeting wearing a Celtic top, local Sinn Féin councillor Colly Kelly has pledged to wear more appropriate attire in future.

'It's a disgrace that he even had the cheek to turn up in a football top in the first place!' said Hairspray McLaughlin from Shantallow. 'Imagine going out

in public like that, never mind to an important business meeting!' she added before shuffling off down the frozen food aisle in her Spongebob Squarepants pyjamas.

Some locals continue to support Mr Kelly, though, and have set up a Facebook page to demand justice for the cause. The 'G'on, Wise up and Reclassify Sportswear as Smart-Casual' group hopes to take the issue global.

'We're a bit disappointed with the low level of support so far, but hopefully we can still get the message out there,' said the man behind the campaign.

'Maybe *Pure Derry* could even give us a wee mention in one of its articles?' he said before running off down the street wearing a black tracksuit top over a granda shirt.

'Gotta run now, buddy, late for a job interview!' he shouted.

It is thought that Mr Kelly will now attend all council meetings wearing a full-size Fozzie Bear outfit, priced a reasonable £99 on the Jim Henson Workshop website.

'Wacka wacka!!' said the council worker when we stopped him for a comment on the issue.

Other headlines

Derry sports store is robbed three times in shocking daylight robbery. 'Fuck 'em ... now they know what it feels like,' says Derry mother.

Altnagelvin statistics show that 73 per cent of Derry women have successfully used their personality as a form of birth control.

Drama as City Paints refuses to sell a roll of wallpaper to two-time Irish presidential election loser Dana Rosemary Scallon. 'I can't even get backing for my wains' school-books,' she complained.

Dear Majella,
I've been starting to feel like a bit of a weirdo lately because I have developed some unusual habits. I'm a thirty-four-year-old single fella, and I haven't had much luck with the ladies in the last few years, despite the fact that my mum always buys me nice clothes and I've got the biggest bedroom in the house. I can't work it out at all.

Anyway, I've been getting a bit desperate lately and going out to pubs to perv over women. Sometimes I rub up against the really hot ones at the bar, sniffing their hair and even stealing the straws from their drinks to try and get a taste of their lipstick. I feel dirty the next day, but at the time it's exciting!

Dear Majella

DERRY'S #1 AGONY AUNT

Anyway, lately I've developed a habit of getting Folly Cabs to drop me off early on the way home, so I can sneak into the neighbours' gardens and sniff any underwear on the clothes lines. Is there something wrong with me? I feel like a total sicko.
Yours,
Sockstash McCafferty

Majella says
Naw luv, I use Folly Cabs the odd time too, they aren't as bad as everyone makes out. Don't be so hard on yourself. We all have to get home some way or the other. Chin up, pet.

Majella

DERRY MOVIE CHART

In another feature brought brilliantly to life by our fans, we asked the *Pure Derry* community to re-imagine famous movies with a Derry slant. Like before, there are just too many of you funny fuckers to mention individually, but some of the suggestions were utter brilliance. Well done to everyone who got involved in both the suggestions and the Photoshopping. Our favourites, in no particular order (ok, I lied, the best ones are at the end), are …

36. The Spide Who Loved Me

35. The Diamond is Forever

34. The Sorcerer's Apprentice Boys

33. Docs Shop and Two Smoking Barrels

32. The Madness of Fort George

31. Big Trouble in Little Diamond

30. Indiana Jones and the Raiders of Moss Park

29. The Da Vinci's Code

28. Sex n' the City Hotel

27. Nightmare on Elmwood Street

26. Journey to the Richmond Centre of the Earth

25. Noel King's Speech

24. Schindler's Pissed

23. Paramilitary Activity

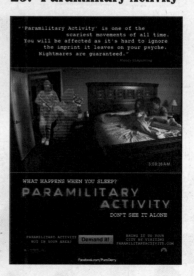

22. **Ballymac to the Future**

21. **Sparface**

20. **RAAD Santa**

19. **The Magnificent 720**

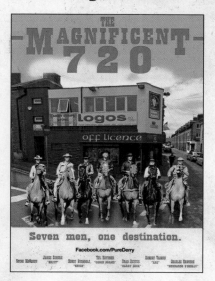

18. **One Flyover the Cuckoo's Nest**

17. **Charlie and the Shirt Factory**

16. **Doherty Dancing**

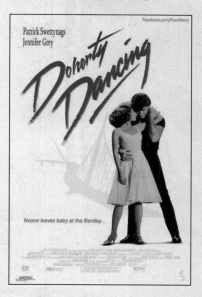

15. **Bookie Nights**

14. **Herbie Goes to Bananas**

13. **Raging Bull Park**

12. **There's something about Mary B's**

11. **When Harry Met Scally**

10. **Madagasyard**

9. **Derry Maguire**

8. **Little Miss Sunbed**

7. Full Denim Jacket

5. 21 Pump Street

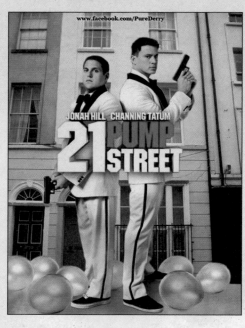

6. The Devil Wears Primark

4. D.L.A Confidential

3.   P.S.N.I Love You

1.   Yes Lad

2.   Friends With Housing Benefits

Runners up ...

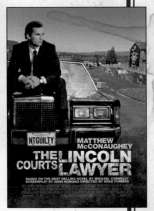

Pure Derry

Too cool for school (well, on a Sat and Sun anyway)

SHOCK AS DERRY PEOPLE FIND SOMETHING TO COMPLAIN ABOUT

Derry whingers came out in force yesterday as news of a proposed new development at the former Tillie & Henderson site emerged.

The shameful plans, which include not having a fuck-ugly pile of rubble at the entrance to the city any longer, were revealed to the press in a computer-generated impression of the site, clearly showing a new white shiny build-ing in the place of a fuck-ugly pile of rubble.

'It was bad enough that they burned down such a horrible-looking building which repre-sented the good old days of sweat-shop labour conditions in a bygone era,' said local house-wife Apron McCallion. 'But now, to add insult to injury, they announce that they plan to bring lots of well-paid jobs to the city too!

'What a disgrace!' she added.

Not everyone was disap-pointed, though. Hundreds of pigeons that were made homeless when the factory was destroyed were said to be delighted at the announcement. The homeless birds have been living rough since that fateful day, begging for scraps of foods at Water-loo Place and Guildhall Square. Feathers McCafferty, a third-gen-eration homing pigeon, was overjoyed at the news, taking time out of his busy schedule of shiteing all over people to talk to *Pure Derry*.

'Tillies was our home and we were gutted when it burnt down. We always warned poor Squawk about smoking them fag butts in bed, but, Jesus, would he listen? God bless his soul!

'Anyway, we have been down and out since then, living rough on the streets and taking shel-ter in old rundown buildings such as the Richmond Centre. It's been getting that bad that we were even considering taking a house up in Ballymac!' he admitted. 'But hopefully this new development will provide shelter for us finally.'

The new building, which will cost somewhere in the region of £26m to finish, will house a fully licensed hotel, a complete enter-tainment complex including a twelve-screen cinema showing nothing but soap operas, a three-level gymnasium dedicated to BootCamp and Polercise, two bookmakers, a Celtic megastore and a five-storey P.J. Bargain-booze pub.

A source close to the project defended the new controversial building design. 'We had terrible problems getting proper authentic materials from the era when poverty-stricken Derry women were making shirts for rich cunts in America, so admittedly the new design doesn't have the same feeling of heritage. However it does pay homage to Derry's historic role in the NASA space programme.

'We know how much the shirt industry meant to Derry,' he continued, 'but on the other hand, look at how badly everyone took it when they all relocated to Asia to exploit new emerging economies and take advantage of child labour!

'You wouldn't even have thought anyone had lost their job, such was the selfless concern for the poor children!' he added.

DERRY KIDS TOLD 'FIGHT FLAB, NOT EACH OTHER'

New alarming obesity figures released last week reveal that Derry kids are shockingly overweight and out of shape compared to past generations.

Government health officials poured into inner-city housing estates this week to investigate, initially causing panic in many areas.

'The residents here aren't used

News shorts

Council chiefs are playing down reports that a woman was seen drinking in a city centre bar on Sunday afternoon dressed inappropriately. The mystery lady, supposedly a visitor to the city, wasn't wearing six-inch stilettos or a mini skirt at the time of the incident. Reports suggest that a number of local women intervened to apply an emergency tan, fake nails and hair extensions, allowing her to enjoy the rest of her quiet Sunday like a normal person.

The Brunswick Cinebowl has declared the 5.30 a.m. premiere of *Batman: The Dark Knight Rises* an amazing success following ALL screens selling out for the super-early event. 'It was brilliant!!! I'd normally be fast asleep by that time,' said Crossword Doherty, who works nightshifts in Seagate.

Foyle Meats shocked as thirty Polish workers walk out after Pope insult. 'We're disappointed,' said a union representative, 'but at least they didn't take the Mr Sheen and feather dusters with them when they went.'

The new housing benefit reforms continue to anger many Derry residents. Young housewife Plasma McCool claimed that she would now find it near impossible to keep up mortgage payments on her husband Mickey's house, which they moved into together in 2010 following their 2009 separation.

to seeing men in suits,' said Grainne Goodthing, a trauma counsellor based in Ballymac. 'The last time was in 1987 during the famous "wrong turn" incident, which resulted in hundreds of residents putting TVs in wardrobes and hiding under beds.'

Parents shocked by the report have come out defending their corner, claiming they have done no wrong. 'We buy the best of stuff from Lidl every week, sometimes spending up to £2 or £3 on fresh fruit and vegetables, but it doesn't seem to make a difference,' said Aine Plate, a seventeen-year-old mother of five. 'My oldest boy, Morgan Levi, goes through waist sizes so fast it's scary. He is actually getting too big to do sport or exercise now, so he has to wear tracksuit bottoms and football tops all the time as they're the only things that fit him.'

Health officials, though, pointed to lack of exercise as the main cause of the problem, claiming the alarming usage of quads, mopeds and scramblers is directly proportional to the high number of fat kids in these areas. New legislation to ban motorised transport in Derry housing estates as a result of this investigation was slammed by local mothers.

'My wee Donzo uses his quad so much he hasn't used his legs in years,' said Michaela Mi Wadi McLaughlin from Carnhill. 'We'll have to get him a wheelchair if this law goes through. It's a disgrace!'

DERRY DHSS TO INSTALL WHEELCHAIR ACCESS

News has emerged that the Derry DLA Office will soon commence the construction of a wheelchair access ramp and general upgrade of facilities for disabled citizens.

Speaking to *Pure Derry* yesterday, spokesman Ignatius Haircut added, 'We cannot rule out the possibility that, at some point in the future, one of our customers may have a physical disability of some nature and we need to be prepared for that eventuality.'

Mr Haircut continued, 'It is only good fortune that has seen a steady stream of able-bodied people come through our doors as our other Northern Ireland branches have been dealing almost exclusively with disabled customers.'

DERRY MILK BOTTLE FACTORY LAYS OFF TWENTY-FIVE STAFF

Management at the Derry Milk Bottle Factory have this week been forced to make twenty-five staff redundant following their worst summer of business for over thirty years.

Gordon Davidson, head of the Milk Bottlers Union said, 'Summer demand this year has been atrocious. For some reason, Derry people used to go through a lot of milk bottles in summers past and we had to replace them, but that's not the case any more.'

Managing director of the factory, Gregory Campbell, was devastated by the lay-offs, but claimed he had no choice but to let people go. 'We just aren't making the same profits we used to. I know all of the unfortunate staff personally – some of them are taking it really bad, especially Trevor, Sammy, Peter, William and Farquhar.'

A recent effort by Mr Campbell to drum up some support for the beleaguered factory fell

flat on Saturday past when he invited some friends down to rally for the cause. 'I invited a few dozen busloads of friends and colleagues to attend a rally

through the streets of Derry in support of the factory,' said Campbell. 'We were hoping that the young people from the Bogside and Creggan would have turned out in bigger numbers to help fight and secure a big order for the factory. We are obviously disappointed that didn't happen!'

In a last-minute announcement, Littlewoods have come to the aid of the redundant staff with an offer of part-time employment at their Waterloo Place store. 'We had a few million put aside for our annual fire damage renovations but no one even bothered setting us alight this year, for God's sake!' said store manager Fanta Bradley.

'Raging!' he added. 'I usually head to Santa Ponsa for a week with the missus.'

Dear Majella,

I hope you can help me. I'm a forty-two-year-old man who has been living with the same woman now for many years. We have a nice house, decent jobs, a good car and live a comfortable life. I suppose I can't fault her – she would do anything for me – but lately I've started thinking that we need some time apart. Even that I should move out altogether.

One of the girls at work has been flirting with me, sometimes texting me – and it's really turned my head. I've found myself making excuses for coming home late, just so I can go for drinks and spend some time with her. I'm starting to really fall for her. I got caught texting her over breakfast yesterday and got the third degree, as you can imagine. Thankfully I managed to talk my way out of it.

Anyway, I am starting to feel guilty now and really freaking

Dear Majella

DERRY'S #1 AGONY AUNT

out about how I'll break the news at home. Is there any way to tell a woman you want to make a clean break without causing her to flip out or hurt her feelings??! She is my Ma after all.

Regards,
Doherty McLaughlin

Majella says

Holy sweet Jesus fuck! Men like you sicken my shite. That's your poor Mammy's house and you should've moved out of there years ago instead of sponging off her and taking advantage of her good nature. You should be ashamed of yourself.

It's no wonder most Derry women think all men are bastards. You remind me of my loser of an ex-husband. He was always going on about how much he loved his Mammy. If it wasn't for the fact he was still paying the mortgage on my house that he bought, or giving me child support money every week, I probably wouldn't even let him take the wains.

I let him, though, cos that's what good mothers do – every single weekend. Now sort yourself out and stop taking advantage of your mammy just cos she loves you.

Majella

Pure Derry

Take your oil, hi. Emergency drums starting from £15.

News shorts

Pampers' scientists 'completely baffled' during recent roadshow appearance in Derry, upon discovering that local kiddy piss actually is blue. Pub chain P.J. Bargain-booze was quick to distance itself from the findings, claiming that local stocks of blue WKD had been bought by customers who were 'most probably definitely over eighteen'. Meanwhile, thousands of local parents claimed their children were all safely staying over at a 'wee friend's house'.

Politicians rejoice as direct underground gas line from Belfast to Derry nears launch. Speculation that similar engineering innovation could someday yield a straight overground Belfast–Derry train line rejected as 'pure fiction'.

BBC NI offers Derry City Council alternative city centre camera infrastructure following CCTV 'switch off' threat. 'We might not necessarily be much help enforcing the law, but Jesus it would be great entertainment!' said a spokesman.

CANDY TO BLAME FOR DRAMATIC WEIGHT LOSS

Childhood obesity levels the world over are reported to be dropping drastically, as mothers everywhere neglect their children in favour of playing mobile puzzle game, *Candy Crush Saga*.

'Ummm hmmmm,' agreed concerned mother of three, Teresa Appfordat, when we asked her whether she thought the kids eating out of the kitchen bin behind her needed a proper meal.

'Sorry, be with you in just one second,' she added.

'I haven't eaten takeaway now in two months,' said a slim-line Jake McKeever, aged six.

'Actually, I haven't really eaten anything …' he mused, '… unless you count that weird blue stuff that was under the sink.'

'Mum, what was that?' he shouted repeatedly, to no reply.

Worldwide grocery sales have slumped for the first time in a decade, as purchasing extra lives, additional moves and unlocking new zones on the Candy map has taken priority over household budgeting.

'I used to get called "Porky" at school,' said eight-year-old

Tammy O'Rourke. 'But thanks to the new "fuck-all-squared-meals-a-day" diet plan my mum has me on, I'm no longer getting bullied!' she beamed.

'Although my mum did elbow me in the face last night for licking her iPad,' she added wistfully. 'Them wee sweets just looked so lovely though.'

It's not just kids who have been affected by the epidemic. Men everywhere have noticed a huge decrease in sexual activity, causing scientists to postulate that there will be a massive decline in birth rates in late 2013.

'JUST MOVE TO COLERAINE' PLAN UNVEILED

Derry residents were last night preparing to evacuate the city and start a new life in lands afar, as the Derry–Belfast railway line was dealt yet another blow.

'Ah for fuck's sake I haven't gotten a bit in weeks!' moaned Frisky McCafferty, a thirty-four-year-old IT manager. 'I managed to fool her into sex about a month ago by screen-printing a Candy Crush puzzle onto a pair of boxer shorts … but when I tried again a few nights later, she just complained that she'd already completed that level.'

Employers are now warning female job hunters that competence in online puzzle games should not be added to your CV or resumé.

'But I'm on level 227, for fuck's sake,' moaned irate genius Stacy Summers on her unsuccessful application to become an attorney at a distinguished local law firm.

'It's a disgrace after everything I've achieved in my life,' she continued. 'I'm going to email the fair employment people and make a complaint …

'… right after I finish this level I'm stuck at!' she added, before returning to her phone for several hours.

Despite spending a figure reportedly in the region of a 'clean fortune' on a fleet of new trains, including the acquisition of three new crisp flavours for the snack trolley, Translink has announced further service reductions on the troubled line. This has the literally dozens of Derry people who regularly use the premium quality, high speed, super efficient, well priced, regularly running service worried that the end is nigh for the Derry to Belfast line.

'We are now recommending that everyone moves to Coleraine!' said Jim McSpokesman from Derry City Council.

'It's a real shame, especially given the effort that Translink have went to in recent years to provide a decent rail link between Northern Ireland's two major cities. All that sterling effort seems wasted now.

'Ah well, I must go pack my house up,' he added.

Coleraine residents were said to be not so keen on the idea, though, especially given the bad feeling between the two towns. Bannsiders have long resented being burdened with building a new Ulster of University campus in the 1960s, at a time when Derry could easily have been lumped with the hassle instead.

'We have had nothing but heartache since that fucking university was built,' said Coleraine resident Gerry Bumpersticker. 'I wish they had built it up in Derry instead. We never wanted that monstrosity and we don't want them Derry hallions now either.

Some people prefer to stay positive, however, such as local traffic warden John McJohnsly. 'I don't particularly like Derry people, but I wish people in

Other headlines

Shock as Derry taxi arrives on time during a premiership football match.

Uproar as Catholic church in Derry found to be fiddling with the books. 'It's a disgrace,' said Gregory Campbell, 'but it's a welcome change of tack.'

Local woman quits while ahead after winning £10 on a National Lottery scratch card. 'I just spent all my winnings in B&M Bargains accessorising my entire living room. My gambling days are over!' she said with glee.

Coleraine would stop complaining about that fucking university being built here. We have had to endure forty years of complaining and it's getting really tiring. It's time to stop blaming the social and economic problems here in Coleraine on us getting that poxy world-class learning facility.

'You would almost think we were feeling sorry for ourselves!' he added.

It has been rumoured that, should the train service be cancelled, Translink's emergency back-up plan will involve the scheduling of buses to Belfast every fifteen minutes from Foyle St bus station. However Translink were quick to dismiss this as fantasy.

'That's just ridiculous,' said Translink representative Foncy Swivelchair O'Hara. 'If there was really that kind of demand for people to travel between Derry and Belfast, do you not think we would just improve the train service?'

One avid train user, seventy-six-year-old Bert McIntyre from Belfast, was really disappointed at the news when we caught up with him boarding the connecting Derry-bound train at Coleraine Station.

'I have been travelling on the Belfast to Derry line for over forty years and I think it would be a total disgrace to scrap it now,' he said.

When asked how he thought the loss would affect Derry, he said, 'I don't know, to be honest. This is still my first trip.'

ENGLISH SPORTS FANS DELIGHT AT ACTUALLY WINNING SOMETHING

Following their recent historic loss against Northern Ireland at football, English sports fans can once again rejoice in the knowledge that they have been reaffirmed as world leaders in *something* as they celebrate a historic win against Australia at cricket.

Man of the moment Freddie Flintoff, an assured future winner of the BBC 'Which Sports Personality Can We Gloat Most About Taking Credit For This Year'

Awards, is set to be honoured with the erection of an eighty-five-foot statue in London's Hyde Park next month. The statue, which will portray Freddie in a lifelike cricketing pose, will be constructed entirely of Lego and built by public well-wishers and journalists.

'Aside from being easy to construct,' said one journalist, 'in the highly likely event that it doesn't hold out against the extreme pressure placed upon it by ourselves and the public in the coming years, then it will be easy to dismantle too.'

Dear Majella,

Is no one else of a similar mind to myself that the *Derry Journal* has been committing acts of reverse discrimination against Derry's middle classes by publishing pictures of shameful council estate debauchery in the 'It's my Party' section of its sister paper, the *Foyle News*??

Too long have les yeux of the nouveaux riches of this town been subjected to extensive coverage of yet another christening, complete with underage parents, gaudy drapery, terracotta bakes, and hair straightened and streaked to within an inch of its life.

There is high-class entertainment to be had outside the bowling alley, although you would never realise it from looking at the *Foyle News*!

When will we see a two-page spread devoted to one of the Dine and Dance extravaganzas that are held in Da Vinci's on a Saturday night? Or coverage of the Captain's Day Dinner Dance at the City of Derry Golf Club? I can guarantee that sales of this particular rag would treble if such events were covered, and not least because the revellers featured in the photographs would put their hands in their pockets and actually buy the paper instead of stealing out of the Central Library!

Majella, what can be done to address the continued bias towards the great unwashed and

Dear Majella

DERRY'S #1 AGONY AUNT

unworked of this town in our local newspapers?
Regards,
Raphael Westlake McCartney

Majella says

Listen, luv, I dunno what your problem is, but you obviously haven't been to any of the swanky parties I have been at. I'm talking voulevants, chicken goujons and boiled eggs cut in half with mayonnaise and lettuce – the whole works.

Most of the pictures hanging up in our house came from the *Journal* or the *Derry News* party sections, I'll have you know, so I won't hear a bad word said about them. Ye see that wee code printed below the pictures in the paper? Well do you know what that's for??

Well neither do I, to be honest, but if you run the scissors just above it so you don't leave any of the text, you can pretty much cut out the whole photo to keep for yourself. Couple of picture frames from Mighty Price later and, I'll tell ye, you will have yerself one hell of a swanky photo collection.

My granda actually uses that OutLastNite to trace our family tree ye know. It's far better than the Heritage Centre by a mile. I found hundreds of relatives through it, including two wains I didn't know about, who were out drinking in the Carraig Bar last Sunday.

Anyway, you need to chill out a wee bit with the snobbery. I have friends who live in posh places like Hazelbank, Shepherds Glen and them flats down in William St, but I don't treat them any differently, and it works both ways. It's all about respect. Why don't you write a wee i-mail to the *Derry News* and ask them if they would consider including youse next week?

If it's any consolation, I'm sure you could have something printed in your local parish bulletin. Its dead easy to organise, I seen it on *Emmerdale* one night! Just slip a few sly score notes to the priest in the pub (and let's be honest, you have no shortage of them) and you will be sorted.

Majella

FUNNIES

Weddings

Socialising

Protecting The Community

Flying The Nest

Cultural Exchange

Customer Service

Pure Derry City FC

Red and White Army

News shorts

Felix Healy was unavailable for comment today regarding his steadfast insistence on continuing to grow a moustache. Moustaches, which were once the hallmark of any self-respecting Derryman, have become increasingly unpopular in recent years. Indeed, anti-moustache protests have become an increasing problem in world sport. F1 driver Nigel Mansell, who famously switched to Indy Car following a hateful campaign of moustachism, remained tight lipped on this new development, though admittedly it was hard to tell.

A new dynamism will be available to defensive stalwart and City legend Peter Hutton on Thursday night, after co-defenders Clive Delaney and Sean Hargan rallied together to buy the fifty-year-old tackle supremo a car for use on the pitch. Hutton, sixty, has been complaining all year of a lack of mobility, and City hope that his brand new 1995 Renault 19 will allow him greater speed in tackling and control on corners. Diehard fans will of course remember a similar scheme under which Pascal Vadequin operated from the right wing on a plough, some fifteen years ago, when Hutton was just seventy-four-years old.

McCOURT IN DOGGING SCANDAL

Scandal has hit Derry City FC this week, as local soccer superstar Paddy McCourt was discovered taking part in a seedy 'dogging' session by a *Pure Derry* undercover team.

McCourt, 24, a native Brazilian who signed for City from River Plate last year, was caught red-handed taking part in the sleazy shenanigans in Sainsbury's car park.

HANDCUFFS

McCourt – who came to City as part of a record-breaking golden-handcuffs deal involving two tenners, a bag of spuds and thirteen Spanish exchange students from the Foyle Language School – was busted by police shortly after our undercover team struck. McCourt was left even more red-faced when he was found to have a bag of Sainsbury's groceries in his car boot containing questionable items including balsamic vinegar, extra-virgin olive oil, sushi, Greek hummus, Camembert cheese and rocket lettuce.

GAGGED

McCourt has officially been silenced by his bosses at the club, who have banned him from

speaking publicly about the incident. However, we caught up with a woman involved the sordid affair, who was happy to tell us about McCourt's performance. Twenty-three-year-old Polish girl Aine Bachyabich, an aspiring glamour model and actress who wished to remain anonymous, told *Pure Derry* that McCourt was amazing but sometimes frustrating.

'He was brilliant for the first forty-five minutes. His touch was amazing,' she said. 'But as the crowd gathered to see him perform, he didn't quite live up to the early flair he showed. It's a shame he can't perform like that all the time, or he could easily be one of the best shaggers in the world.'

TIED-UP

Derry manager Stephen Kenny was unavailable for comment on the issue, as he was otherwise engaged in important meetings in the build-up to Paris. However, others did come forward. 'We are really disappointed in Patrick,' said one former friend. 'It's a big shock to everyone and we all feel let down by him. It's really embarrassing.

'We thought he was a sausage-roll-bap man like the rest of the squad. But fucking rocket lettuce! ... Jesus H. Christ!'

Sorry, the deal was only City til you DIED.

Other headlines

Rumours of a long-awaited sequel to popular Derry police documentary dismissed despite appearance of *Derry City Beat: Again* in leaked BBC schedule. 'It's actually a new programme of extended highlights from the Brandywell,' said a source.

Following his departure from the club, Derry City fans have applied for planning permission to build an 'Eddie McCallion Tribute Wall' at the Brandywell, marking his incredible fifteen-year contribution to the team. If successful, the forty-foot high wall will be positioned on the eighteen-yard line of the pitch, just in front of the home nets.

HEART-THROB BREAKS A THOUSAND HEARTS

Thousands of Derry women had their hearts broken this week when Derry City FC defender and local heart-throb, Eddie McCallion, tied the knot with his long-time sweetheart.

Whilst hundreds of McCallion's friends, family and well-wishers turned out to give the newlyweds their blessing, *Pure Derry* can reveal that a crowd of weeping women congregated at the Brandywell to mourn the loss of such a fine specimen.

McCallion, last seen by a source at *Pure Derry* running on a treadmill at a local fitness centre for five-and-a-half hours, gave no indication that he was due to be blessed by the vows of holy matrimony. He did, however, according the group of girls gathering at the reception, look great in a powder-blue Nike T-shirt and shorts ensemble.

McCallion, regarded by many as one of the most attractive men in Derry, was not available for comment on how he got to be so handsome. However, a source at Altnagelvin Hospital did reveal that an unusually high number of attractive males were born in and around the period of McCallion's birth.

'It's a phenomenon,' said senior nurse Attracta Tension. 'Usually the babies born over here are either wile-looking or at least hit too many branches when they fell out of the ugly tree. However, that fateful night, for some divine reason, God graced us with a plethora of infantile beauties, and young Eddie was one of them.

'I still have his baby picture on the inside of my locker,' she added, whilst staring lovingly into space and clasping her chest.

One man – who was born only a few hours after McCallion, and is, according to reports, just as, if not even more handsome

than the local footballing hero – was tracked down by *Pure Derry* through our sources at the *Mirror*. Whilst wishing to remain anonymous, the man did take the opportunity to wish McCallion and his wife all the best in their new life together, and promised

to buy him a beer the next time he seen him.

City Council officials have opened a book of condolence at the Guildhall, aimed at bringing some closure for the literally thousands of distraught women who have been rocked by this tragedy.

BANDYWAGON PRIDE

Local shops are reporting dangerously low stocks of Lenor following Derry City FC's monumental victory over Shelbourne to reach the FAI cup final.

Washing machines across the town are said to be working hard to wash mildew and musty smells from vintage replica Derry shirts, as diehard fans, who haven't been near the Brandywell for years, look forward to a big day out in Dublin to support their local team.

Elsewhere, Altnagelvin's A&E department has been inundated with loyal Derry fans who have

fallen foul of step ladders and attic doors whilst trying to locate their beloved DCFC memorabilia.

'Raging with meself!' said Fleccy McColgan, as he cradled a broken arm in a sling fashioned from an old Derry scarf. 'I was convinced my 50-ft "Spirit of Treble Winners '89" banner was behind the water tank, but I couldn't find it!'

'Although I did find Felix Healy,' he added with a smile. 'He was over behind the Christmas decorations reading the oul match-day programmes. Me and him sang a few karaoke numbers before I got carried away and went straight through the plasterboard into the wain's room!'

Derry beat Shelbourne 0–3 at Tolka Park to secure a place in the final – a statistic which made thousands of passionate local fans extremely happy when they read it on Facebook afterwards.

'I'm made up!' said Creggan McCusker from Pennyburn when we spoke to him walking through Rosemount on his way to the Bogside to catch a lift to Shantallow. 'We've a 53-seater bus organised to head down ... and 36 of the seats are held over for carryout space! Canny wait!'

The only real concern for Derry is the loss of star supporter Gary Jamieson who has gone on holiday to Vietnam, leaving the Candystripes with a real selection headache in the stands. The in-form City supporter had been on fire recently at the Brandywell, with a match average tally of starting 8.5 'City Til I Die' singalongs per match.

'We'll miss that level of firepower,' said manager Declan Devine. 'But I feel we've got the experience to cope.'

The final will be staged in Dublin's Aviva Stadium on Sunday 4 November. Fair weather is expected.

DERRY BUSINESS COMMUNITY GOES ANTI-FRENCH FOR BIG MATCH

In the build-up to the big match with Paris Saint-Germain at the Brandywell, Derry's business community has rallied together to instill some anti-French sentiment into their products in the name of civic pride.

Taking their inspiration from the American craze for 'Freedom Fries' in the wake of French opposition to the proposed Iraq invasion, Derry's business elite has begun their own propagandistic renaming of foodstuffs feared to have a French bias – starting with chips.

Residents throughout the Bogside and Creggan are now raving about the brand new 'Liam Coyle Spirit of 1993 Double-Winner Super Fries' flooding chippers throughout the Maiden City, while you can't move yards from any of the city's fancy restaurants without hearing mention of the snazzy new 'City Til I Die!!!' Dressing.

Additionally, the Bridie's chippy chain has stopped selling chicken goujons because 'they sound too French!' and also ceased the serving of Bollinger champagne because 'it was probably a fuckin' stupid idea to stock that in the first place'.

'Hopefully this will be less controversial than the time we banned Scotch Eggs for the game against Raith,' said owner Bernie Mouth.

Not every move, however, has been so graciously accepted, as the city's teenagers are said to be somewhat unenthusiastic about adopting the terminology 'Peter Hutton kissing'.

LAST TANGLE IN PARIS

Furious Derry City fans have hit out at Parisian officials today for refusing to build a grassy mound adjacent to the Parc Des Princes stadium from which they can watch the return leg of the big PSG match for free.

'I canny believe I have to buy a blooming ticket! It's ridiculous!' said local City fan Denim McLaughlin. 'I'm going to have to get a loan off the Credit Union when I get back to pay for all this now!'

French police are believed to have removed a large group of Derry fans from the Paris City Cemetery, after a group of early arrivals set up camp at the graveyard in the hope of gaining a vantage point from which to watch the match.

The men initially refused to move from the graveyard, despite being told that the stadium was actually four miles away. Police were left with no choice but to forcibly remove the men, who still angrily insisted that they would eventually 'find a decent angle' from which to watch the game for free.

This follows news that Parisian residents living around the stadium have been complaining for days about groups of beer-swilling Derrymen standing in their porches, climbing trees and shimmying up lamp-posts in the area. More to follow.

Pure Scary

Happy Hallowe'en

THE SICK SENSE

A group of Hallowe'en thrillseekers, who were staking out a haunted house in Carnhill, hoping to catch a glimpse a famous local ghost, got a massive fright this week when the spectre never bothered to turn up for work.

The nameless ghost bride, who usually appears in the window of the haunted house on moonlit nights, has gone on the sick recently, adding to an already alarming rate of absenteeism in the ghost community.

Last month, residents living in the Lowry's Lane area were shocked to not see any sightings of a legendary priest's head rolling down the hill, causing immediate panic in the community.

This follows a frightening experience for Rosemount residents, in which an evil headless horse disappeared shortly after being really nice to a group of drunks leaving the Village Inn. Local taxpayers are now up in arms about the situation, disgusted at the notion of funding the laziness of layabout ghosts, who are seemingly intent on sponging off society.

A source close to death hinted to *Pure Derry* that the town was now seeing a full-on ghost strike fuelled by bad working conditions citywide. Local ghosts, who have been walking through walls and appearing at windows for several generations around the city, have sadly had to endure years of tacky renovation work recently by house-proud Majellas.

'It just doesn't have the same scary effect when I walk from the kitchen into the living room through glass partition doors,' said one ghost in Creggan.

'And to make it worse,' he continued, 'they have built an extension outside of the house now too and took away my window. Ye can't really scare people through them Veluxes! It just looks a bit silly!

'Though I did startle a pigeon last week,' he happily reflected.

People in communities all over Derry are now reported to be secretly meeting at each other's houses under the cover of darkness, to tell each other terrifying ghost-less stories and swap frightening tales of ghostly disappearances.

The City Council – which is currently backing several ghost trails around the town, such as the Hallowe'en Bus Tour and the Toucan One Fright Cruise – tried to play down the fiasco, claiming that Derry 'still had plenty of scary sights'.

Alternative tours to Frankie Ramsey's, the Telstar, John St and Moss Park are now thought to be in the planning stages.

I can't be arsed with this today. Would love a sausage bap.

TODAY
FRIDAY
13

CITY COSTUME CHAOS AS HALLOWE'EN LOOMS

Pure Derry has learnt that the city will face a major costume catastrophe over the next few days, with rabid locals bleeding the clothing racks dry as we write.

The tribulations arose when several clothing alteration shops citywide decided to close their doors to new business, due to an excessive demand on their services.

'A Stitch in Time doesn't really save nine,' said Mary O'Cotton from the Waterloo Street outlet. 'In fact, we're so busy these days, it's probably gonna cost you a tenner extra!' she cackled as she over-locked a pair of dangly cotton ballbags onto a moose outfit.

Many people in the city are now believed to be looking towards more conventional types of costumes, and there have been reports that some charity shops have had their shelves stripped bare in the run-up to Hallowe'en.

'It's a disgrace,' said Fenderstrap McCorduroy, a local musician and Bound For Boston regular. 'Me and my mates have been to every charity shop in town and we can't get a single bloody thing to wear.'

News shorts

Dracula believed to be responsible for two dozen male bodies found throughout the city drained of blood. A local right-wing feminist group has welcomed the attacks, claiming they will teach Derry men to wind their necks in.

Dracula later claimed body count would have been three times that figure if it hadn't been for the ridiculous volume of garlic chips consumed across the city this weekend.

Gotham billionaire Bruce Wayne dramatically fled Derry this week after a local criminal mastermind somehow figured out his secret identity during a business trip to the Province. Marty McLaughlin, a Tesco employee, maintained his innocence in an interview with *Pure Derry*. 'I was only being polite like, ye know what I mean, Batman?'

Reports suggesting that some tourists visiting Derry managed to get a cup of coffee on a Sunday have been squashed by the DVCB as 'vicious rumours'. This sentiment was echoed by the City Council, as they rolled out a new scheme to promote the city cemetery as a hot visitor attraction. 'Derry has always been dead on a Sunday, and we intend to keep it that way!' said marketing guru Curly Denial.

'Eh?' he replied when we asked him what he intended to dress up as for Hallowe'en.

Desperate shoppers citywide have, however, been given hope of late, with the opening of several hundred 'seasonal' Hallowe'en shops in every abandoned retail unit, unused doorway, manky alleyway and large wheelie bin, from Shipquay Street to the Strand Road. All stock a wide range of four types of vacuum-packed costumes, numerous varieties of five rubber masks and several black bins full of cheap overpriced plastic accessories which are destined to be confiscated by doormen three minutes after you get out of the taxi. These shops have promised to make sure no one goes without.

Traditionalists have poured scorn on these shops, though, as the panic for homemade costumes is causing chaos citywide. Uniformed city workers such as street sweepers, binmen and bus drivers are now being shadowed by security guards around the clock, to protect them from gangs of youths intent on stealing their outfits.

In a later rethink, police assigned a further detail of plain-clothes officers to protect the security guards protecting the uniformed workers, who were getting nervous about dodgy looks from tracksuited youths carrying measuring tapes, tailor's pins and packets of Wonder Web.

Shortly before we went to press, there were unconfirmed reports that two alcoholics were stripped and robbed of their clothes in the John Street area.

Police are trying to trace the owner of a pair of size nine Timberland boots and a John Rocha jacket, which were discarded at the scene.

Sport

HALLOWE'EN FIXTURE SPOOKS LOCAL FOOTBALL FANS

Following the 0–0 draw with Sligo in the recent FAI Cup Semi-final, Derry City FC are bracing themselves for a dramatic Hallowe'en night replay of the match at the Brandywell this Tuesday.

Despite putting on a brave performance in Sligo on Sunday, Derry couldn't break the deadlock in ninety minutes, setting up a thrilling spook-tacular showdown at their home ground.

Following this season's poor turnouts at matches at the Brandywell, for which only a mainstay of diehard fans have bothered

to turn up, club officials are preparing themselves for this season's first BIG turnout, thanks in large part to the novelty of the event.

It is now anticipated that thousands of fancy-dress-wearing Derry locals will arrive at the ground on Tuesday, dressed as Derry City Fans especially for the occasion.

'Obviously we are not used this kind of situation,' said City manager Stephen Kenny, 'but, nonetheless, everyone is welcome

along to the Brandywell for the occasion.'

In the event that Derry reaches the final, DCFC has confirmed that two hundred fifty-two-seater coaches are on standby to ferry the hundred members of Brandywell Pride and a small number of hardcore fans and press to the final.

sensation of a good pair of Alan Whickers under his tracksuit?

Please help, Majella. I'm thinking of goin for a G-string under me boiler suit tomorrow. Am I some kind of wackjob?
Confused,
Creggan

Majella says

In a word … aye, ye are. You're fruitier than my Fat Frog, darling. I like a man who appreciates my underwear (you know who yees are), but wearing your wag's nags is not cool. The only time a man of mine has come close to wearing my knickers was when I caught me G-string on Higgsy's bar stool in the Metro. It was sticking up above me jeans, I was trying to get served and he jumped up when Celtic scored. Well, the whole thing ripped off and landed in his pint. He nearly died and I took a total reddener.

Well, apart from last Hallowe'en when Higgsy put on fishnets and stilettos, but he just did it for the craic. He's mad man like that, always up for a laugh! Last summer on holidays, too, he came bouncing around our hotel room

Dear Majella

DERRY'S #1 AGONY AUNT

Dear Majella,
I don't know if this is normal, but women's underwear really does it for me. All those tightie whities, frilly thongs and satin knick-knack-paddy-whacks are too much temptation for a fella to take. I see them on my girl and one big, overwhelming sensation comes over me, Majella. Jealousy!

Why should my girl get to wear all the good underwear, eh? Is it a crime to think that I would look good in silk panties too? So what if a fella wants to feel the

Other headlines

Northern Ireland Electricity promises to fence off all transformers after electrical fire wreaks havoc in Belfast suburb. Decepticons said to be delighted at NIE assistance in the war to capture Cybertron.

Bogside Community Representatives petition the council to force real police officers to wear uniforms saying ACTUAL POLICE for easier identification on Hallowe'en night.

Council announces that a longstanding Hallowe'en tradition is now to become law. Girls are to be banned from the city centre for wearing costumes covering more than the allotted 24 per cent of their bodies.

Council criticised for blowing Hallowe'en budget on one huge firework pointed at Strabane.

Spider-Man is from Derry, claims local woman. 'Well he's a fuckin' creep isn't he?'

with my French knickers and suspenders on, just to get a rise out of me. Jesus I laughed my head off. And the other night when he was trying on my shoes when we were pissed – God, he's such a kidder. All me shoes are stretched with the badun, lol.

So anyway, Confused, my point is that I think you have a serious problem. God love your poor missus, the poor critter probably hasn't a clue! I'm just thanking my lucky stars you're not my fella.
Majella

MAJELLA'S MAILBAG

Jesus, you lot don't half have issues, hi! If you thought I was good at getting full every day, then you should see my postbox. I let the postman come in and empty the bag on me every few days. Anyway, look, I'll be honest, I haven't got the time to answer all your letters, you poor critters. Sometimes though, youse just write in to pass on a wee message, or share your words of wisdom, so I thought I'd print a few of the best from over the years. Take care, me darlings, *Majella*

Dear Majella,
These new sticky stamps are great. Not only does not having to lick them make them a great labour-saving device, but by altering the faces of footballers on old Premier League stickers to make them look more like the queen, you can save on the price of postage whilst getting rid of all those Chris Bart-Williams you have in double. I must have about forty of him. Seemed to be the only fucking player Myra's in Creggan ever sold. In the end I filled in all of Notts Forest and half of Man City with the massive frog-faced twat.
    Yours helpfully,
    Mr Starjump Devenney

Dear Majella,
I wonder if, through your good paper, I can highlight the growing problem of suicide prams around the city centre. I have noticed that when young and not-so-young mothers wish to cross the road, the pram is thrust several feet into the oncoming traffic, whilst dear old Mum is safely on the pad.
    I have had several narrow escapes. Last week I narrowly missed colliding with a Pedigree Mk2, a Maclaren Quest GTI and a Silver Cross Buggy TCDI. All within minutes of each other in and around the Diamond.
    Prams are bad enough, but one can take some solace in the fact that prams usually contain small babies either asleep or blissfully unaware of their mums' take-no-prisoners attempts to get to the nearest bargain.
    However, the terrified faces of the three- and four-year-olds in buggies and pushchairs will haunt me forever. Their little grimacing faces, gritted teeth, the sheer look of terror. Their mothers' behaviour must have a lasting effect.
    I wonder if the violence on our streets at the weekends could be traced back to post-traumatic stress as a result of being wheeled around Derry by Kaga McLaughlin, Soriyu McGinley, Akagi Deery or Paddy Banzi?
    Yours sincerely,
    Concerned Local

Dear Majella,
I took great heart reading the recent *Derry News* article which reported that the North West Institute for Further and Higher Education is set to expand even further and higher. My two grandsons are graduates of the Tech, and without the guidance and support they received there, they would not be as financially secure as they are today. Pool sharking and playing games of snooker for a £1 a head can be quite lucrative when you have been well coached, so I hope that the expansion forges closer links with Maxi Break on the Strand Road and sees further development of the Students' Union recreational facilities.
    Yours respectfully,
    Mrs Pearldrops Hegarty

Dear Majella,
A tip for all those nationalists who, like me, occasionally feel powerless to stop the despicable union with Britain and the heinous influence of perfidious Albion. Using a thick marker pen – the kind one might find in any high street stationery shop – deface the wording on maps and street signs which say 'Londonderry', leaving just 'derry' still legible. Revolted and terrified, we'll soon see those soldiers leave our shores!
Revolution 1–The System 0
Tiocfaidh Ár Lá,
Mr Oisin Mhuinteoir-Mhadagh

Dear Majella,
A tip for any female readers who are unlucky in love: ring up Gerry Anderson's radio show and pretend to be about seventy. The wily septuagenarian can't resist a flirt, you get on the radio and it's cheaper than those mobile numbers you find in the bus station toilets. Happy calling!
Yours helpfully,
Ms Sanction McIvor

Dear Majella,
I would like, through the medium of your good newspaper, to offer a few suggestions to any evil tyrants with aspirations of world domination who may be reading your column. Whilst not wanting to appear condescending towards criminal masterminds of such calibre, I do feel that there is room for improvement in their high-altitude field operations.
For example, when sending several henchmen on a mission to kill a hero or notorious super-spy, and it transpires that he is currently holidaying on a snowy mountaintop resort, I offer this useful but effective advice:
Rather than waiting until the hero has readied himself for a day's fun on the freshly powdered slopes, and then engaging in a pointless high-speed downhill pursuit with machine guns (which often results in the loss of several of your personnel and is quite embarrassing to your organisation), simply order your crew to wait for the hero in the toilets of the hotel bar the night before, and then shoot him whilst he is taking a shit.
Aside from the obvious time saved, I believe this approach will also yield several financial savings for your business, including sparing the need to invest in several sets of expensive equipment, sinister black matching skiing outfits or state-of-the-art snow mobiles. More importantly, according to my contacts at Grafton recruitment, I understand it is becoming increasingly difficult to find reliable and hardworking Olympic standard winter athletes with professional weapons training, so it's only a matter of time before this role becomes obsolete in a criminal organisation.
I hope that some of them will find these simple cost-saving tips beneficial to their business and future world-domination plans.
Kind Regards
Midge McGocks

Dear Majella,
It's come to my attention that the Soda Stream Corporation – manufacturers of the old Soda Stream machines that used to inject fizz into anything you liked – are no longer refilling the carbon dioxide canisters used to power the late-eighties fizz-making phenomenon. I never had one myself, but will be on hand to blow a steady stream of carbon dioxide into the metal tubes for any nostalgic, fizz-loving constituents, free of charge.
Yours helpfully,
John Hume

Dear Majella,
My mate Dave says he's depressed, but I find that if I wear ladies' clothing and enough make-up, and run up to him making a high-pitched screeching noise, he laughs after a while.
If you ask me, it's all a con.
Yours perceptively,
Mr Keyboard Dineen

Dear Majella,
While watching *Derry City Beat* for the past few weeks, I have greatly appreciated the BBC's music producer choosing gangster rap to play during any section in which a police car moves through a troublesome area. For too long the connection between the stone-throwing of the Bogside's ten-year-olds and the triple-figure body counts and weekly fatal shootings of LA's gangland has been overlooked. Thanks, BBC, for subtly implying the manifold similarities between the two areas that I would otherwise never have spotted myself!
Yours gratefully,
Mr Horizontal McLaughlin

Pure Derry

Pure Decommissioning

News shorts

Unionist disappointment continues as IRA ceasefire rages on. Much dreaded decommissioning of deadly weapons now expected within weeks.

175 job losses at Adria will put Strabane into a '1950s-like recession' claims Sinn Féin spokesman Ivan Barr. 'I agree,' said local UUP councillor Gordon Bleu during a rare show of political unity. 'It will set us back at least ten years.'

Ian Paisley attacks SDLP leader Mark Durkan claiming that he is 'blotched with fascism'. Mr Paisley, a member of the Orange Order who was jailed twice in the late 1960s for opposing civil rights reforms, was today unavailable for comment.

'Paisley is a sad desperate old man,' said Durkan later, 'and anyway, what has my dress sense got to do with anything?' he asked.

Gregory Campbell has hit out at the remembrance of Operation Motorman, claiming nationalists continue to live in the past. 'Unionism is all about looking forward into the future, and always has been, right far as back as the Battle of the Boyne, and before,' said Campbell.

CONSTRUCTIVE TALKS UNDERWAY

Stormont Construction Ltd is in deep crisis, it has been revealed, as redevelopment of the government-funded 'New Society House' falls drastically behind schedule.

Local plumbing sub-contractor Sinnk Frame are being blamed for the problems, which started when leaks were found coming from areas they had been working in. Sinnk Frame denies this, though, claiming they are the victims of collusion by clerk of works David Trimble and the Plumbing Service of Northern Ireland.

'The PSNI have always had it in for us, ever since we claimed their organisation was notorious for producing bent copper,' said Martin McGuinness, head foreman of Sinnk Frame.

TOOL TIME

'Of all the contractors on this site, Sinnk Frame has worked the hardest to achieve a total restoration of all services within this building,' he added.

It is believed Sinnk Frame was unhappy with New Labour conditions at the development, often finding wires in many of the areas they were working in.

Now retired John Hume, an architect who worked on the original plans, admitted that the development was in trouble. 'It's chaos in there!! No one is speaking to each other, they are building walls where there should be doors, and the place is freezing due to all the cold water the trade unionists keep pouring on everything. We need to create institutions that respect diversity but

ensure that we work together in our common interest. Once this is done and we break the airlock, the real heating process will begin.'

Mr Joe Public, who hired Stormont Construction Ltd to carry out the work on the property, is understandably annoyed at the lack of progress on his house. 'They have had the same framework up for six years and still haven't made much progress except for the occasional provisional modification. It's getting beyond a joke now – I'm pissed off waiting about for these people to do something while I pay their wages. It's a shambles!

'There is only one extension lead on the whole site, and no one will let Sinnk Frame use it. They just don't seem interested in shar-

ing power with them,' he added.

Despite the setbacks, David Trimble is reportedly pleased with some sub-contractors, including the Ulster Union of Plasterers, who have successfully plastered over the cracks that have been appearing at his offices recently following a dispute with the Decorative Undercoat Painters. Sinnk Frame blamed the problems on a shortage of Trade Unionist Joiners.

PD NOTES: Published on *Pure Derry* in 2005, seven years after the Good Friday Agreement, in response to the lack of actual progress on devolution. Tensions were high after Sinn Féin alleged their cars and phones had been bugged by British Intelligence.

DISSIDENT ATTACKS CONTINUE DESPITE DECOMMISSIONING

Police have made appeals for calm amidst a recent wave of criminal activity by angry, unarmed republican dissidents.

Rogue paramilitaries have been witnessed engaging in criminal activity up and down the Province, with thefts, assaults and intimidation all reported despite the organisation's lack of weapons.

On Wednesday a terrifying attack on police was witnessed in South Armagh when six men climbed out of a black taxi and pelted a police station with tomatoes and peas before driving away. As yet no group has claimed responsibility, but police say leading republicans have been

spotted with 'catapults and/or pea-shooters' sticking out of the back pockets of their shorts.

Police have linked the attack to the same gang responsible for a score of other incidents since Tuesday's decommissioning. As early as Tuesday night, several witnesses spotted a gang of dissident republicans making 'bomb noises' and shouting 'big mortar attack!' in the direction of several army barracks in Derry and Tyrone.

On Thursday, a gang of men held up the Ulster Bank in

Strabane using what have been described by police as 'very detailed' drawings of handguns.

'This new unarmed faction is seemingly without shame or remorse,' said Huge Ordeal, chief of the PSNI. 'This was proved by their cowardly attacks on members of the DPP this week.'

The police chief was referring to the torment suffered by Sheila Montgomery from Coleraine's District Policing Partnership, who was followed by a group of 'very sarcastic masked men' who repeated everything she said for three days.

'BRING BACK INTERNMENT' DEMAND LOCAL DIY STORES

Huge job lay-offs at DIY superstores Budget DIY and B&Q are expected to be announced today, as the pressures of trading in a new peaceful society take their toll.

'Ever since that fella Seamus Doherty got released from prison we have been struggling like hell,' complained Noel Backscratcher of Budget DIY. 'Our paint department sales have dropped 500 per cent since that dreadful day. We used to shift mountains of that cheap white vinyl silk, but it seems no one is interested in it any more!'

Pete Moss of B&Q echoed these concerns, claiming that more would need to be done to ensure secure employment in branches all over NI. 'Lets face it,' he said, 'the golden days of internment were great for everyone. Kids in the Bogside had something creative and constructive to do with their days. Tourists were flocking to numerous gable walls across the city to marvel at our rich heritage and spelling mistakes. Local paint businesses across the town were thriving and jobs were abundant. The repercussions of this will be enormous.'

Indeed the shockwaves are already being felt at several other businesses around the town. Padraig Bomberjacket, Chairman of the Bogside Hopelessly Shite Graffiti Initiative and author of classic Derry graffiti such as 'Ian Paisley is a smelly bum' and 'Don't shoot me I'm a Brit' phoned *Pure Derry* to complain.

'What are we supposed to paint on the shutters of the Credit Union now, eh? This peace process malarkey is a con! Even our Mickey down the cleansing department is losing his job over the head of it. Sure what's he supposed to clean up now? We too had to let several staff go. The signs for the future are not looking good,' he said.

'Well, in fairness, our signs never looked that good in the past either, but ye know whadda mean lik!' he added.

News of the recent arrest of Martin 'Ducksie' Doherty for failing to give evidence at the Bloody Sunday Inquiry brought a small glimmer of hope to the many unfortunate businesses and persons caught up in this dreadful saga. Pete Moss of B&Q added 'We might be able to offer a few part-time contracts on a temporary basis if that one works out, but it's hardly enough. The sooner we get back to proper internment the better, as far as I'm concerned!

'Who knows, though – we might get lucky and get a few dirty protests out of him. Repainting a cell numerous times could be quite lucrative!'

IRA IN 'KILLING PEOPLE IS WRONG' SHOCKER

The Birmingham pub bombings were 'wrong and should not have happened' Sinn Féin has announced.

A party spokesman said last night that he'd woken up on Tuesday morning and realised it had been 'a bit lousy'. Party spokesman Padraig O'Flynn said 'We'll get onto the blower to the IRA as soon as possible and let them know that we've worked this out. I can't believe we didn't realise sooner!'

The statement came just before the thirtieth anniversary of the two bombings which indiscriminately killed twenty-one people and injured nearly two-hundred in the Mulberry Bush and the Tavern in the Town pubs in November 1974.

According to *Pure Derry*'s source, the statement 'did not say in so many words that the IRA will apologise but I'm sure that's what they meant. And sure that'll be the end of that and all the relatives can finally rest easy.'

The IRA has apologised in recent years for a number of murders it carried out in the 1970s. It only took them thirty years, but the general populace are said to be glad they've finally seen the error of their ways. Mr O'Flynn said, 'Better late than never and all that, even if the victims won't be around to hear it.'

In October, the republican organisation issued a 'statement of regret' for killing an entirely innocent fifteen-year-old boy with the mental age of an eight-year-old in Belfast in 1973. Mr O'Flynn said, on behalf of the erstwhile 'freedom fighters', 'He looked much older. He could easily have got a carryout. Or into a nightclub even. Well he could have up in Derry at least.'

Last year, the IRA apologised for the grief caused to the families of the nine so-called 'Disappeared' who were murdered and secretly buried on beaches and in bogs back in the 1970s. Unfortunately they couldn't give the whereabouts of all the bodies due to having had 'a few too many pints of the black stuff back then'.

'Jaysus, C company were wile men in them days,' he added.

In July 2002, the IRA apologised to all civilian victims of its campaign of violence. The apology was so well received that a number of the deceased even voted Sinn Féin that year.

Court reports

A round-up of court appearances in the Derry area from our local crime reporter, Eavesdrop Harkin.

A nineteen-year-old man from Derry was convicted on Thursday of repeated loitering over a period of six months in music shop Cool Discs. The offender was described as routinely entering the store pretending to browse – occasionally picking up products, humming approvingly and scratching his chin – but never intending to buy. His counsel said that he was merely trying to appear cool while waiting for lifts outside the bus depot. He is up in court again next week for allegedly making frequent trips into the Central Library solely to use the toilets.

Further loitering charges were lodged against a rag-tag bunch of self-proclaimed 'misfits' who were witnessed several times over the past year outside Iceland, usually in skater gear. All were found guilty and, in summing up, the judge sentenced the pretentious teens to five years of mandatory 'wising up', effective immediately. Should the defendants be judged to be suitably wise after six months, they will receive a lighter two-year sentence of 'catching themselves on'.

To great excitement the IRA was arrested last week after foolishly signing his name on a wall in Waterloo Place. The IRA was

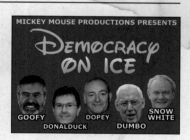

MICKEY MOUSE PRODUCTIONS PRESENTS

DEMOCRACY ON ICE

GOOFY   DONALDUCK   DOPEY   DUMBO   SNOW WHITE

revealed to be John McLaughlin, 15, of Culmore, who pleaded guilty to the graffiti charges but denied that he was in fact the renowned illegal terrorist organisation. The judge did not accept his claims and duly sentenced him to more than two-hundred thousand years in prison for a plethora of deaths, bombings, beatings and robberies over the last forty years. Sinn Féin has declined to make a statement on the matter.

Pure Derry

It would freeze the balls off a brass monkey.

News shorts

Facebook PLC is bracing itself for a busy day tomorrow, as tens of millions of its part-time weather forecasters excitedly prepare for snow. Upon the announcement, stocks in 'Looking out the window' fell sharply for the fifth consecutive year.

Outrage in Derry as snowfall fails to deliver promised levels of white, freezing misery in the North West compared to other parts of NI. 'Them c**ts up in Belfast get everything first!! It's disgraceful,' complained Scratchy Duddy from Creggan.

'… and them BBC weather forecasters are a joke too! It's hardly worth dodging the TV licence man any more for fuck's sake!' he moaned before quickly shutting the door to avoid the window cleaner.

Gregory Campbell calls for Equality Commission to investigate appointment of Monsignor Eamon Martin as coadjutor Archbishop of Armagh. 'Not another Catholic!!' moaned Campbell. 'Once again no Protestants were considered for a top job in Northern Ireland.'

'EVERYONE FAMOUS NOW A PAEDO' SAYS HOME OFFICE

The British Home Office has just confirmed that, as of 5 p.m. today, every celebrity in the entire world will be listed on the UK Sex Offenders' Register.

They hope the move will help save costs and reduce administration overheads for everyone.

The change means that the Register will now switch to a new revolutionary 'opt-out' system, whereby it assumed that everyone famous is a paedophile until they come forward to say otherwise.

It affects everyone who has ever had a career in television, radio or media, and is intended to save the general public time in deciding which famous person that they've only just met to leave alone with their kids.

The move was met with horror at all major television networks and left children's TV presenters across the board with the difficult task of trying to explain hours of footage of them clearly standing in the same room as kids – sometimes wearing little more than a jumper and a pair of jeans.

However, not everyone felt the same. A group of former *Big Brother* contestants, the cast of *TOWIE*, and every woman who has ever appeared on dating show *Take Me Out* today picketed the Home Office, demanding the right to be considered paedos too.

Many journalists across the UK are distraught at the news, especially tabloid showbiz columnists. It is feared that their entire catalogue of 'Wicked Whispers' clues for the next twelve months can now be answered by randomly selecting anyone ever seen on TV.

Home Secretary Theresa May was unavailable for comment as she was at Scotland Yard removing her name from the list before picking up her kids from school.

DERRY RESIDENTS UNSURE WHETHER 'WEST-SIDE STORES' EVER REALLY EXISTED

Citizens of Derry seem to be confused as to whether or not their town had a so-called 'West-Side Stores' in its recent past, or ever at all, according to a report by Bogside University.

'On the one hand,' said interviewee Hammersmith McDaid, 'I seem to remember there was a big supermarket there after Stewarts left. Or was it Crazy Prices? I don't remember exactly, but there was something there before Tesco anyway, and it was something to do with West Side, aye.

'On the other hand, however, the idea of a massive supermarket themed around the frontiers of America in the mid-1800s seems a bit insane.' McDaid isn't alone in his confusion at the idea. Derry's city planners only discovered blueprints for the centre four years ago amid bewilderment and scepticism. 'It says that it was here, definitely, for at least two or three years, maybe more, around about 1995–97. But, were that true, surely more people would remember it, and more importantly question why in the name of massive cocks was there

a supermarket which displayed a giant cowboy mascot called West Side Sam. Why would anyone have shopped there?'

The poll also highlights that residents have other ideas for what may have been there before Tesco. 19 per cent of those asked suggested Harrods and 12 per cent thought 'some kind of roller disco'. Forty-three per cent, however the overwhelming majority believed it to have housed the Ghostbusters HQ. 'Aye, that Ghostbusters place, wasn't it?' enquired Mrs Pyjama Quigley of Creggan. 'Sure we used to be swamped with the oul ghosts, back in the day. Egon was a mucker of mine.'

Added Quigley, 'Cheeseburgers were only 20p then.'

'NIGHTLIFE IS BAD FOR NIGHTLIFE' CLAIM LOCAL NIGHTLIFE KINGPINS

Up to five Derry bar owners have lodged a complaint about a planned Christmas market beer tent at the Guildhall Square.

Five bars in the area – including The Metro, Downey's Bar, The Monaco, The River Inn and Tracey's – have all complained that it would affect their own ability to sell handsomely priced alcohol this Christmas.

Downey's, in particular, deserves our pity for this tragedy, having previously been awarded the contract to run the extremely busy on-site bar at the Clipper event. It is thought that the proximity of Downey's to the Guildhall Square in this instance, however, means the owners now 100 per cent dislike outdoor beer tents.

The former chairperson for the Institute to Eternally Monopolise Bar Profiteering in Derry has been in touch with *Pure Derry* to have his say.

'We are naturally all for culture coming to Derry!' he said, 'provided it conforms to our own code of conduct – to only add value to our bank accounts and not the city itself!'

He said he'd be taking the opportunity to further document his thoughts in a brief 4–5 page editorial piece in the next issue of the *Derry News*.

Owners of bars around Belfast's City Hall were said to be bemused by the drama, as they have successfully stayed in business for several years alongside their own Christmas Market.

It is thought that the Roads Service has now been asked to look into improving the time it takes new concepts to travel over the Glenshane to Derry, as the current waiting time of seven to ten years is proving unacceptable.

Showbiz

Proud Derry ice-cream van Mr Whippy today posed for pictures for assembled press, after the van won the latest edition of *The X-Factor*.

Mr Whippy chose a rendition of 'Pop-Eye the Sailor Man' for his accompanied piece for last Saturday's show, finishing with a rousing instrumental of *The A-Team* theme tune to win the hearts and minds of the audience both in the studio and all over the UK.

Louis Walsh was said to be delighted that such a great Irish talent had once again done well in another fabulously credible talent competition, even suggesting that Mr Whippy could go on to emulate the success of other Irish superstar, Mickey Joe Harte.

'Mr Whippy was brilliant up there – I couldn't take my eyes off the performance. Except for

when I was blinking and twitching,' he said.

'Actually, I hope someone at home recorded it – I'll probably have to re-watch it later,' he admitted.

Sharon Osborne, whilst obviously reeling from the defeat of her second-placed protégé 'Nokia 3210', did wish Mr Whippy all the best and admitted it had been a great performance. Rumours romantically linking the winner to her daughter Kelly surfaced when the van was allegedly overhead trying to woo her with promises of a '99-er with a Flake'. This was flatly dismissed by Mr Whippy, though, who reportedly said he 'wouldn't poke her if she was the last girl on earth'.

The van has also won plaudits from credible music press for tackling social issues, reminding his fans to 'Mind That Child' just as Coldplay's Chris Martin reminds his to 'Make Trade Fair'.

Music industry insiders now speculate that the long awaited *Flintstones* themetune project may actually come to fruition. Likewise, a much-hoped-for rendition of *Scooby Doo* was still an unconfirmed rumour at the time of going to press.

Dear Majella

DERRY'S #1 AGONY AUNT

Dear Majella,
I've always had my suspicions about my best mate's girlfriend but said nothing because I know how much he loves her. The other day, though, I got home early and decided to nip round and give back a few CDs I'd borrowed, when, to my horror, I discovered her shagging some complete stranger on the kitchen table! When I confronted her about this she laughed and said my mate would never believe me over her 'cos she has him wrapped around her wee finger. What should I do?
Regards,
Nervy McGilloway

Majella says

I see you're taking your mate's part in all this. I have to say I'm not wan bit surprised, typical man! Let's face it, you don't know what he's like to live with, sure he might be the best of craic in the bar, but for all you know he could be a right head-doer in the house, and could be shite in bed. I suggest you keep your nose out of it and let the wee girl have some fun – God knows she deserves it.
Majella

Dear Majella,
A year ago, I caught my girlfriend cheating on me. When I confronted her, she promised she would never do it again and I forgave her. Since then, though, I have caught her twice more – each time she has promised never to do it again and I have forgiven her.

I don't know what I am doing wrong. I am a good bloke – I even give her half my wages to keep her going during the week. But lately she has been distant and going out with her friends more than normal. I am starting to think she is cheating on me again. What's your advice?
Thanks,
Combover McGroarty

Majella says

Only HALF??!!! No wonder she is riding someone else, for God's sake. There is no such thing as a 'nice bloke' either – you are all bastards! Don't try and tell me you've never had a bit on the side. Of course you have. You are a man, and you're all cheats and liars! Dry your eyes, mucker.
Majella

Pure Merry

It's beginning to look a lot like Christmas.

SNOW SURRENDER

Northern Ireland became the laughing stock of the world again over the weekend, as diehard Christmas fans violently protested over the news that Belfast's Christmas tree was no longer going to be on display for 365 days of the year.

Christmas trees, which are only erected over the winter festive season in the rest of the world, have been a year-round fixture at Belfast City Hall for many years. However, a recent democratic vote on the matter has seen Belfast follow in the footsteps of Lapland and adopt the same Christmas tree policy as Santa himself. Nevertheless some Christmas fans think it's still an affront.

'It's an utter disgrace,' said loyal Christmas lover Billy Knuckleson. 'I am Christmas through-and-through, and I demand that my insecurities on the matter are reassured at all times by the year-round display of a Christmas tree at City Hall.'

When we explained that not even Santa has his Christmas tree up all year round, and that Belfast is now equal to the North Pole on

the matter of erecting a tree, he seemed unmoved.

'I don't care for your rational and reasoned mumbo jumbo,' he barked. 'It's nice to be equal with our beloved Lapland naturally ... but we expect to be MORE equal.

'God Save Santa!' he shouted finally before rejoining a group of men burning a Christmas tree to make their point about how we should respect Christmas trees.

Santa, who was watching the saga unfold on TV at his winter palace at the North Pole, was said to be disgusted at the sight of spides rioting in the name of Christmas.

'These rioters don't represent the good name of the Christmas empire I reign over!' he said.

'Plus, if they have a valid point, why do they have their Christmas scarves covering their faces?' he asked one of his elves.

CHRISTMAS SONGS ARE OUT OF TOUCH

'Rudolph the Red-Nosed Reindeer' is 'insensitive and sets a bad example to children'.

These are the findings of an investigation carried out by an independent government watchdog, tasked with taking everything too seriously and removing the fun value from anything that hasn't already been spoilt.

Mr John Turndull of the National Organisation for Frightfully Unsuitable Narrative told *Pure Derry* that 'Rudolph' – and indeed many other Christmas songs – were setting a bad example to young children all over the world. '"Rudolph the Red-Nosed Reindeer" is a shockingly inappropriate tale of prejudice, discrimination and elitism,' said Turndull. 'As we all know, none of the reindeer would accept Rudolph for who he was, but instead used to laugh and call him names based on his disability. They refused to allow him into their inner circle and, as such, wouldn't let him join in any reindeer games. This xenophobic and cruel depiction of Santa's

reindeers is a shockingly gruesome and inappropriate story to tell young susceptible children.'

Mr Turndull continued, 'Admittedly Rudolph was eventually accepted into the group after proving his worth and becoming "cool", but as we know from our previous studies of other heinous works such as *Pretty in Pink* and *Teen Wolf*, this acceptance comes at a price. I mean, let's look at the facts. He only became a valued member of the group when Santa

News shorts

Confusion amongst Derry sixth-form students as council launches new Christmas 'Park & Ride' service. 'Sure haven't them fellas who park outside Smyths toy store been running that all year?' asked one.

Council money-saving idea backfires as Santa makes incredible list of demands for turning on the Christmas lights. List thought to include 2 white sofas, 15 bouquets of lilies, 3 plasma TVs, 5 baskets of fresh fruit, 14 cases of Evian, 8 packs of Stella and a platter of freshly made sausage-roll baps. 'That's the last time we'll get Mickey from the cleansing department to dress up as a favour!' grumbled council marketing whizz Curly Denial.

Eamonn McCann has hard time explaining idea of 'property as theft' to his young child at Christmas dinner. All the boy wanted was an iPod Touch. Oddly-shaped fair-trade wood carving from Africa proved not as popular.

and the other reindeer NEEDED something from him. They realised that Rudolph, with his nose so bright, was the perfect candidate to pull the sleigh that foggy night, and so offered him the hand of friendship. But they didn't want his friendship! They were obviously just using him!

'Where was Santa when Rudolph was isolated and rejected? Where was Santa when he had no one to play with and needed the love and support of an adult? Are these the horribly material and selfish values we want to instil into our children? I think not!'

Mr Turndull's list of inappropriate songs will be published in a report which will soon be submitted for discussion in the House of Commons. The outcome could see many Christmas songs altered or re-recorded to suit the proposed guidelines. Although this report is still top secret, Mr Turndull did offer *Pure Derry* an 'exclusive' insight into some of the songs put forward for alteration.

'Rockin' Around the Christmas Tree', the 1958 classic by Johnny Marks, promotes unsafe behaviour in modern day society according to Turndull, due to the risks of epileptic seizure from the lights, the commonly occurring hotchpotch of poor electrical wiring, and the tendency in modern homes to have cheap laminate shiny flooring. Turnbull's suggestions include changing the title to 'Standing Beside the Christmas Tree … with your Eyes Closed … in Appropriate Rubber-Soled Footwear … and Pushing the Tree Safely into a Corner'.

'I Saw Mommy Kissing Santa Claus', the 1952 song by Tommie Connor, encourages the notion that adultery is okay, and gives children false hope that Santa may someday move into their house to become their 'new daddy' and lavish them with gifts every day. According to Turndull, this song should be completely banned from the airwaves, along with similar titles such as 'Why is the Easter Bunny Humping my Mummy?' and 'The Tooth Fairy Took More than my Teeth Last Night'.

He concluded, 'This has gone on for long enough, and something has to be done. How can we expect children to understand that the highly complex underlying social issues that exist in many of these songs are just a bit of fun?'

Some record labels have already begun taking pre-emptive action, by recording alternative versions of some Christmas songs. One such song, Bing Crosby's 'White Christmas', was re-recorded by Derry crooner Fergal Sharkey in a secret session in London's Abbey Road Studios last week. So poor was the version, though, that the producers opted instead for a superior set of alternative Bing Crosby vocals, which were obtained in a Los Angeles recording studio shortly after digging him up.

MAJELLA'S GUIDE TO LAST-MINUTE CHRISTMAS SHOPPING

Yes hi, what about ye?

There is no escaping a bit of last-minute Christmas shopping up the town. Some of ye will have forgotten a few essentials, some of ye may be busy looking after a sick relative or working, but most of ye will just be men. And men, as we all know, are fuckin' useless!

I'm a dab hand at last-minute shopping, so I've put together a wee checklist for ye all to keep you right when you're up the town this year. Hope it helps.

Good luck shoppers!

1. Forget your mobile phone at home.

Contacting people when you're up the town is over-rated. If I were you, I'd leave your mobile phone at home and leave yerself no means of getting in touch wi anyone. You won't need to check sizes, colours, allergies or none of that shite. Ye'll be grand!! They are just a shower of ungrateful bastards anyway.

If you can't do that, then at least make sure your battery is flat or you have no credit or something. For those of you with contract phones … actually, fuck's sake, what I'm I talking about? It's Derry! Never mind.

2. Don't bring any gloves.

Toughen up for God's sake! Are ye a man or a mouse? Having warm hands whilst walking about in freezing cold is a pleasure that you will not have time for. There is shopping to be done. For me, an essential tradition of last-minute Chrimbo shopping is being so cold that you'll go into any oul fucking shop to get a heat, and end up buying the biggest pile of shite just to stay warm. I buy most of my best presents that way.

If you do bring gloves, don't panic, luv. Just remember to forget to take them off whilst at the phone box trying to fiddle with coins to call the house after you realised you forgot your mobile phone. This will fuck you right off and you'll be ready to kill dead things in no time!

3. Don't plan ahead.

Planning of any kind is pointless love, trust me. With any luck, you'll buy all the heaviest items first without bothering your hole to think about the consequences. Wrestling flat-pack furniture from around the town while you pick up other smaller stuff is half the craic of Christmas for me. Plus, if ye've followed step two correctly and forgot your gloves, you won't just be fucking cold, the bags will be cutting into your hands like fucking cheese wire too! And who doesn't love a bit of cheese at Christmas? Yummy!

4. Overlook the fact that your bank card has a daily withdrawal limit.

If you have done everything properly until now, well done luv. But if you really want to have a proper Derry Christmas, then forget about needing enough cash to cover yerself up the town. In my experience like, the best way to do that is to forget the fact that your bank card has a daily withdrawal limit. When you remember, you'll be panicking like fuck, wondering why ye didn't come into town sooner and lift money out over the counter, calling yourself all the bastards of the day. Ha!

Before you know it, you'll be downgrading everyone's presents and making compromises all over the place. But trust me, you'll save a clean fortune! Everyone will think you're a cheap cunt on Christmas morning like, but ye know what? Fuck them! I do this every year. It's the only way I can afford to get out five nights in a row over the holidays.

5. Don't worry about how you will get home afterwards.

Now that your shopping is done and you are ready to get yerself home, don't beat yourself up too much that you forgot to organise a lift beforehand. Ye'll be grand! Derry has loads of slow-moving taxi ranks to choose from, all with queues of freezing people holding flat-pack furniture. Be prepared to get wile annoyed at how slow it's moving, throw the head and walk off in a huff to the next taxi rank. This will set you up nicely for coming back five minutes later, when you realise the queue you were at wasn't that bad after all, and that the person who was behind you is now at the front.

Trust me though, luv, all of this will be worth it when you get home long after teatime. Sure now you can tell your Mammy how 'black' the town was, how 'shite' Christmas is, and how you can't wait for it all to be over! Just like her and your Da do!

Everyone complaining and whinging together as a family, in peace, love and harmony. Just like Christmas should be. I'm so excited now!

Merry Chrimbo folks!

Love,

Majella.

50 THINGS TO DO IN DERRY

1

DRINK A CARRYOUT UP THE WALLS. The consumption of alcohol atop our ancient and treasured city walls is a long-standing rite of passage for local teenagers. Also a well-known fornication spot, the hallowed walls were the place of conception for 34 per cent of children born in Altnagelvin in the 1980s.

RELEASE A SHOPPING TROLLEY BACK INTO THE WILD. Trolleys begin their lives high in the Canadian Rockies, before swimming into the Atlantic where they are cruelly captured and set to work in the many supermarkets of the world. Local environmental activists are famous for their continued efforts to free them from captivity and release them back into the waters of the Foyle.

2

EAT AN AUTHENTIC SALAD BAP. Derry people will eat most things inside a bap, but never more enthusiastically than when it's a random assortment of iceberg lettuce, soggy tomato, mayonnaise and half a boiled egg. Some dining connoisseurs even add ham to this culinary tour de force. It is rumoured that André Michelin invented his restaurant star-rating system whilst eating one in the Foyle Street bus depot.

3

A **Pure Derry** publication

With thanks to

 DerryPhotos

TAKE AN ARTY PHOTOGRAPH OF THE PEACE BRIDGE FROM A JAUNTY ANGLE. Amaze your Facebook friends with your artistic talents by posting a quirky photo of our new-new bridge on your wall. Choose from a range of mist, frost, snow, fireworks, moon, stars and car headlights to get that extra sparkle in your masterpiece. Maybe she's born with it; maybe it's a self-anchored suspension bridge.

4

5

6

DRIVE AN EIGHT-MILE ROUND TRIP TO SAVE 70P ON FUEL. As local taxi drivers will never tire of telling you, cars are never-ending money pits of desperation and gloom, requiring constant sacrificial offerings to appease the dark lord of motoring. Thankfully, due to currency fluctuations, you can save entire pence per litre by driving several miles out of your way when filling up.

PUT 100 QUID INTO A POKER MACHINE TO TRY AND WIN THE 25 QUID JACKPOT. That £25 payout is yours and don't let anyone tell you any differently! You deserve it, and everything coming to you, for your tenacity and downright dogged determination to extract less from a machine than you put in. There's no 'i' in team, but there are two in idiot, and you like those odds! Go get 'em tiger.

50 THINGS TO DO IN DERRY

7

CLAIM FOR WHIPLASH. Ach, sure, everyone's at it, you might as well bog the arm in too. Simply feign a sore neck the next time someone nudges your bumper in close-quarters traffic, (nearly spilling your coffee) and BOOM, an easy few grand! While you're at it, why not take up complaining about the rising price of car insurance too?

8

BUY THE *DERRY JOURNAL* TO FIND OUT WHO'S DEAD. Nothing makes a woman feel more alive than those spine-tingling, adrenalin-pumping few seconds after figuring out that people who aren't them are dead. Mammies across the city have been passing this ancient knowledge through the ages to new generations of women.

9

EAT TOBACCO ONIONS. (Not that you'll have a choice.) Following the passing of the Fried Onion Amendment Act in 2010, every eaterie in Derry is now required, by law, to serve two kilos of tobacco onions with every starter, main course and dessert. The Northlands Rehab Centre has had success in weaning junkies off the delicious cremated vegetable – known to be more addictive than crack cocaine – using small doses of Tayto Onion Rollers and electro-shock therapy.

10

PRETEND YOU'VE GOT NO ODDS. Street drinkers are chancers who will stop at nothing to get their hands on your hard-earned cash to fund their filthy habit. When they approach you, simply pretend you are skint by shrugging your shoulders and tapping your pockets gently, before escaping into a nearby pub for a well-deserved pint.

WALK UP CREGGAN HILL EATING A PIZZA AFTER TWELVE PINTS OF HARP. Work off those extra calories whilst you eat, using Derry's patented 45° uphill nutrition plan. It is estimated that 22 per cent of Paolo's pizzas are ingested by weirdly angled drunken locals who spent their taxi fare home on food.

11

MAKE A DICK OF YOURSELF IN THE PHOTO SECTION OF A LOCAL NEWSPAPER. It will seem like a good idea at the time, but when your double chin is preserved forever on the sacred pages of a local rag, you'll soon wonder why you bothered gathering all your mates together for a photo between rounds of Aftershock. Extra marks for appearing with someone wearing bunny ears.

12

13

SMOKE A 'SINGLE' FROM DOC'S SHOP. One of the oldest bastions of single smoking in the nine counties of Ulster, Doc's Shop has been providing a 'Spare-Odds-To-Cigarette Conversion Service' for generations. Feargal Sharkey was famously smoking a single from Doc's the night the riff for 'Teenage Kicks' was born. He still owes Mickey Bradley 10p for it.

TAKE A TAXI 200M DOWN THE ROAD. Typically the mainstay of local women, this ancient practice has been amusing local taxi drivers for years, as awkward shoes, laziness and drunkenness combine to encourage the express route to the next pub. Men caught up in these scenarios are arguably more stupid, as they usually get caught to pay too.

SAY HELLO TO A STRANGER. Derry has long been regarded as one of the friendliest places in the world, due mostly to our incessant need to offer gracious salutations to strangers on the street. It comes in many forms, but the patented side-head flick with accompanying 'all right, hi' manoeuvre is undoubtedly the most popular.

14

15

THINGS TO DO IN
DERRY

50

IGNORE SOMEONE YOU'VE KNOWN FOR YEARS. The energy required to offer limitless hospitality to strangers is demanding. To compensate, Derry people save their power reserves by ignoring people they actually know. Start by friend requesting someone on Facebook, then walking past them in the street. A timeless classic.

16

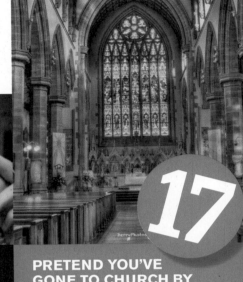

17

PRETEND YOU'VE GONE TO CHURCH BY BRINGING HOME THE PARISH BULLETIN. Although technically a sin, any system which involves repeating the same process every Sunday, until the end of time, is a prime candidate for truancy. Derry kids figure this out early, spending their time playing in the park but bringing home some tangible proof of church attendance.

18

FIX SOMEONE'S BROADBAND OVER THE TELEPHONE. Derry people have been fixing people's broadband over the telephone since before the internet was even invented. Now a full-time career choice for many, an estimated ten thousand people per day from across the world reach someone with a Derry accent on their technical support quest. Most eventually ask to be diverted to India in the hope of speaking to someone they might understand.

This is Your Life

19

LISTEN TO A TAXI DRIVER'S LIFE STORY. Nothing makes a journey with a random stranger so rewarding as the thrill of paying them for the privilege of being their therapist. We, the Derry public, have been counselling our PSV brethren for years through the strife of income tax, mortgages, divorce and parenthood. Alternatively, tell a taxi driver your life story.

TRESPASS ON PRIVATE PROPERTY TO STEAL INEDIBLE UNRIPE APPLES. Whilst the fruit bowl at home will remain untouched, the thrill of scaling a wall, ripping your trousers on a fence and successfully avoiding detection has been making fruit seem cool to Derry kids for generations.

20

21

REPEATEDLY DRIVE AROUND THE DIAMOND UNTIL A PARKING SPACE BECOMES AVAILABLE. Getting a parking space in the heart of the city is great, but if one isn't available, simply circle the roundabout outside Austin's until someone returns to their car. Then, aggressively park behind them, marking your territory by peacocking with your indicator.

GET DRUNK AT THE HOUSE UNTIL MIDNIGHT AND THEN GO TO THE PUB FOR LAST ORDERS. Saving money is an obvious reason for this local practice, but the truth is that most Derry people are so busy drinking and talking shite that the night is almost over before they actually phone a taxi. Most local pubs are quiet until an hour before they close.

22

GET A CRISIS LOAN FOR THE WEEKEND. On paper, your cooker has broken and the wain needs new shoes. In reality, though, you are dying to go on the rip and you spent your last tenner on your weekly shop at Iceland.

Jobs & Benefits

23

SUPPORT LOCAL PEOPLE'S ACHIEVEMENTS RIGHT UP UNTIL THE POINT WHEN THEY ACTUALLY ACHIEVE SOMETHING. Staunchly supporting the efforts of our kinsfolk in all manner of activities is embedded in the DNA of Derry people. Unfortunately, so too is the trait of giving them dogs' abuse once their talents get them places. Use phrases like 'above their station' and 'forgot where they're from' to put such people 'back in their box'.

24

50 THINGS TO DO IN DERRY

25
DO TEN LAPS OF THE METRO BAR ON A SATURDAY NIGHT. Going around in circles is a favourite pastime of us Derry wans. When we aren't circling the Diamond looking for a single space (see #22), we can usually be found circling the Metro looking for a single face.

26
COMPLAIN THAT AN OTHERWISE EMPTY SUPERMARKET CAR PARK IS 'RAMMED' BECAUSE THE THREE ROWS CLOSEST TO DOOR ARE TAKEN. Positioning your car as close as possible to the entrance of your intended destination is a competitive sport in Derry. Indeed local drivers regularly park so close to the door of Sainsbury's that the trolley collectors there are on commission from the Guinness World Records organisation.

27
DO A WEIGHT LOSS BOOT CAMP FOR TWO WEEKS, THEN GIVE UP. Impress your friends by becoming an overnight fitness and nutrition expert. Simply attend a few boot camps, eat a couple of three-bean salads, and boom, fully qualified! Your pals will love hearing about your daily dietary intake in precise detail, and will be genuinely inspired by your 6 a.m. Facebook check-ins for roughly three weeks, before you quit. Honestly …

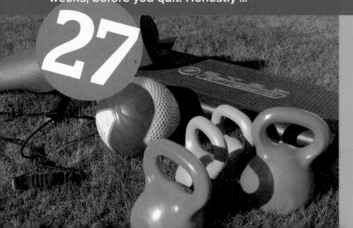

28

GO TO A HOUSE PARTY AT 2 A.M. WITH PEOPLE YOU'VE NEVER MET BEFORE. Hanging out with the same people all the time is dull! So, after the pub has closed, why not invite yourself to a random person's house and stand in their kitchen all night, apologetically drinking their beer from the fridge? Actually, I think they have some vodka in the cupboard too …

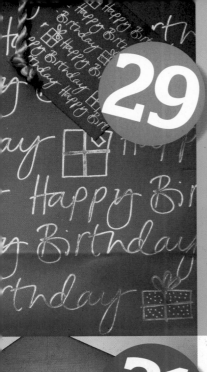

29

GET A 'HAPPY BIRTHDAY' MESSAGE FROM THE SDLP'S PAT RAMSEY ON FACEBOOK.

Embracing social media like boss, SDLP stalwart Pat Ramsey famously dispenses countless birthday greetings via Facebook each and every day. In this, he is following the lead of the great John Hume, who for years went door-to-door giving people the bumps.

30

SKIP THE QUEUE AT BRADLEY'S TAXIS.

You just want to get home, and that massive queue of three-hundred people, all swaying in the wind and eating curry chips out of a nosebag, goes on forever. Oh look, there's yer man, what's-his-face, from two years ahead of you in school, up near the front. Wonder what he's at with himself this weather …

31

GET INTO A FIGHT IN THE QUEUE AT BRADLEY'S TAXIS (SEE #30).

Actually living in one of the most coveted ringside seats in Derry, residents of the Sackville Apartments can reportedly command up to £10 each from guests arriving to watch. Classic signs of trouble starting include 'What da fuck are you lukkin at?', 'Are you startin?' and 'What da fuck did ye say, hi?'

32

INSIST ON CALLING IT BRADLEY'S TAXIS EVEN THOUGH IT'S BEEN CITY CABS FOR YEARS.

Adapting to change is overrated. Why bother learning the new names for stuff, when the old ones will do just fine? 72 per cent of Derry Saturday nights still include pints in the Townsman, a bite to eat in Frankie Ramsey's and a Bradley's taxi home.

33

GET SACKED FROM FIRSTSOURCE.

In Derry, going to work to fix people's broadband is almost as popular as not going to work to fix people's broadband. A whopping 66 per cent of the population of the town have been sacked by a call centre, with Job Centre statistics indicating that 'beat your job up your hole' was the most common response to the news of a dismissal.

50 THINGS TO DO IN DERRY

WATCH A DERRY CITY MATCH FROM SKINT HILL. Paying to watch a football match surrounded by Derry fans seems silly, especially when you consider that you can enjoy the spectacle 150m away surrounded by dead bodies. In a desperate effort to stop the swindlers, Derry City Football Club once famously took out an advert in the *Derry Journal*, asking people to stop dying so they could close the city cemetery down.

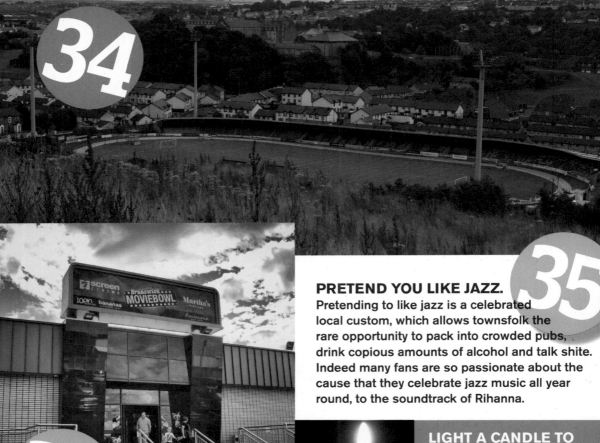

34

35

PRETEND YOU LIKE JAZZ.
Pretending to like jazz is a celebrated local custom, which allows townsfolk the rare opportunity to pack into crowded pubs, drink copious amounts of alcohol and talk shite. Indeed many fans are so passionate about the cause that they celebrate jazz music all year round, to the soundtrack of Rihanna.

36

LIGHT A CANDLE TO BRING SOMEONE GOOD LUCK. A traditional way of asking God a favour, Derry mammies have been lighting candles before important events for years. During the famous 1970s wax shortage, however, local parents were forced to steal candles from the cathedral in order to pray for God's forgiveness.

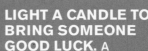

USE THE BOWLING ALLEY AS A BABYSITTING SERVICE.
Spend some quality time with your little darlings in *Pure Derry* style – take them to the bowling alley and tell them to get lost whilst you read the newspaper.

37

38

FLAG DOWN A LATE-NIGHT TAXI USING AN ATTRACTIVE FEMALE AS BAIT. A tried and tested means of getting a cab after dark. Simply ask your leggy friend to stand on a desolate roadside whilst everyone else hides or pretends not to know her. Locals often do this before going to a party with people they don't know. (See #28)

39

EAT A GRAVY RING FOR BREAKFAST. Eating a 'bag of buns' for breakfast is a pleasure that the world beyond our city has cruelly been denied. Derry wans love the delicious taste of a gravy ring first thing in the morning – a delicious baked good that the rest of the world laughably calls a 'doughnut'. Ha, 'doughnut', what a stupid name. Dicks.

40

COMPLAIN ABOUT SOMETHING. Finding negatives in positive situations is a true talent. Through the eyes of such genius, sunshine is too warm, world-class events are too expensive, and vital inner-city regeneration is a waste of taxpayers' money. Sadly, though, none of these brilliant people post on Facebook. Ever.

41

MAKE A DIY COCKTAIL BY MIXING COLOURED ALCOPOPS IN A PINT GLASS. Sadly, bar-staff training in Derry involves learning to pulling pints and taking tops off beer bottles. As a result, locals have taken the ingenious step of making their own cocktails from various toxic-coloured alcopops. Ask a drunk person at the bar how to make a Fat Frog, a Purple Haze or an Orange Order.

50 THINGS TO DO IN DERRY

42

DO THE DOUBLE. There are many ways to get ahead in life, but signing on at the bru whilst working a dodgy cash-in-hand job is right up there. Sadly the dedication and go-getter spirit required to do the double has been lost in recent years, with many unemployed opting simply to do the single now instead.

43

TEXT EVERYONE IN YOUR PHONEBOOK AT 3 A.M. LOOKING FOR DRUGS.
Only joking, this has never actually happened before ...

Contacts
- ☐ Dorts
- ☐ Mackers
- ☐ Pinta
- ☐ Soupy
- ☐ Minter
- ☐ Shumpy
- ☐ Boy from bog in
- ☐ Mackers 1
- ☐ Mackers Creggan
- ☐ Mackers bog
- ☐ Mackers Rosemount

44

GO TO THE PUB TO WATCH AN ENGLAND MATCH IN THE HOPE THAT THEY'LL LOSE.
Many Derry sports fans love going to the pub to watch England matches, in the hope that a team they hate will lose. Thankfully, though, international matches are rare, meaning most weekends are spent watching the English Premier League, in the hope that a team they love will win.

45

QUEUE UP FOR AN HOUR TO TAX YOUR CAR. Despite the fact you can tax your car online or over the phone in minutes, true patriots of Derry are committed to standing in a dull queue for an hour, whilst double-parked outside the Central Library.

46

GIVE A STRANGER YOUR OPINION ON THEIR LIFE AND EXPECT THEM TO FOLLOW THROUGH. Well, 'Person I Just Met at a Party Thirty Minutes Ago', let me tell you where I think your life has gone horribly wrong ...

47

TAP YOUR MA FOR A LEND. Sorry, I actually ran out of electric whilst writing #46. Thankfully my oul doll sorted me out with a tenner til next Tuesday. Cheers, Ma! Alternatively, hit the Credit Union.

48

RELENTLESSLY DRIVE A SOUPED-UP CAR AROUND SHIPQUAY STREET AT 2 A.M. Whilst most of the young men of our town have developed a bad reputation for spending all their money drinking and trying to pick up women in pubs, these upstanding young chaps prefer to pour all their money into petrol, car insurance, road tax and alloy wheels, in an effort to pick up women outside pubs instead. Bravo, gents.

49

DRESS UP FOR A SATURDAY NIGHT OUT, EVEN THOUGH YOU ARE GOING FOR SUNDAY LUNCH. Although mainly a thing that our female residents do, the true beneficiaries of this ancient Derry practice are local men. Taking Mom 'n' Pops out for a quiet carvery dinner, perhaps? Then yes, of course, the six-inch platform heels and mini skirt are the right choice! Why are you even asking?

50

WEAR A FOOTBALL SHIRT TO A JOB INTERVIEW. If you've never sat in traffic and wondered if the guy in sportswear running down the street is out for a jog ... or just someone from Galliagh who is late for a job interview, then you've never really lived! Did someone say 'JJB closing-down sale'?

Thanks

My first and biggest thanks go to friends and family, who have had to put up with this nonsense for years. Or rather, have had put up with me *telling* them about this nonsense for years. Your patience and steely determination not to tell me to shut the fuck up has always been a source of inspiration and comfort. My fiancée, in particular, is to be commended for her resolve in not hitting me over the head with a frying pan during the making of this book.

WRITING

Creatively, my main thanks go to two people, who are both ginger, have almost the same first name, and aren't even related. Seamus McCarron, my best friend of many years, has provided an endless amount of input, feedback and support, and has always been there to bounce ideas off. Seamus was my co-writer on many classic Majella columns, is one half of 'Birdman and Booster Seat' and has even made a cameo in *Pure Derry* as a bouncer priest. Seamas O'Reilly worked alongside me on numerous editions of *Pure Derry* on the original website, penning some truly amazing stories, including 'Phil Coulter in Town Adultery Shocker', 'Orange Order To Buy Bus', 'Derry Community Goes Anti-French' and *many* others. A great co-writer, he is still sadly missed at *PD*. (He didn't die like, he just became a DJ – which might be the same thing.)

CONTRIBUTIONS

Thanks to those who have ever sent us original stories or ideas that we've used or adapted. After a decade, I have doubtless overlooked people, but good folk such as Dixie Elliott, Peter Mahon, Sharon McConnell, Christopher Coyle, Lowman, Enigma and DannyBronco (yes, those are usernames, retro *and* anonymous) have all sent in great stories at one time or another, some of which feature in the book.

Thanks also to all our local footballers, including Liam Coyle, Eddie McCallion, Sean Friars, Darren Kelly and Pat McCourt, for being great sports.

PHOTOS & IMAGES

A special thanks to Christopher Cowan, who travelled the length and breadth of Derry taking many photos that appear throughout this book, and who helped me recreate a mountain of the old corner adverts for print.

Thanks too to anyone who has made their mark on *PD* with their Photoshop skills. Popular competitions such as Derry Movies and so on brought in some brilliant material. We can't mention everyone, but frequent input by the likes of Marty McColgan, Hector McLennan, Emmett McLaughlin, Christopher Cowan, Brian Quinn, Pete Caldwell, GoOnYaBoyYa, AndyP and many others has always been appreciated. Thanks all.

Also, my thanks to Bernard Ward at Derry Photos, who kindly gave up his time and resources to help bring the '50 Things To Do In Derry' feature to life at short notice.

Other photo credits must go to Gary Jamieson (Winter Peace Bridge), Fearghal 'Bergal' Bonner (Dalai Lama), Gareth Hughes (ASBO), Alan Meban (Twelfth Bonfire) and Declan McGuinness (various Derry v PSG).

Lastly, thanks to you for reading, sharing and appreciating *Pure Derry* down the years. (Especially if you actually bought this book instead of reading it at the Central Library.)